Oxford Junior Eng

Oliver Gregory

Illustrated by
John Crawford Fraser
Oxford Illustrators Limited
Edward McLachlan
Peter Kesteven
Martin Cottam
Jennifer Northway

Oxford University Press

Using language

We use language when we speak or write. The written form of a language is very useful because it enables thoughts, ideas and information to be set down permanently and be used over and over again. Nevertheless language is, first and foremost, something that is spoken. It seems certain that spoken language came before written language and this is how, as young children, we learn our native tongue.

a The pictures show some of the ways in which spoken language is used. Write sentences to explain what is happening in each case, suggesting what is being said and indicating how people are using words for a particular purpose.

b Compound words beginning with fore-

Words such as forecast, forefathers, foremost, foreman, foreground, forefinger, forehead, forehand, foretell and forecastle are each made out of the word fore and one other word.

Write the sentences, completing each with a word beginning with fore-.

1   The phrase 'first and _____' means above all else.
2   Simon cut his _____ just above the left eye.
3   A heavy fall of snow was _____.
4   The gypsy claimed she could _____ the future.
5   The artist painted a few flowers in the _____.

c Animal sounds

Write the following, filling the blanks with the sounds that the animals make.

1   dogs _____   6   snakes _____
2   frogs _____   7   horses _____
3   lions _____   8   donkeys _____
4   bears _____   9   oxen _____
5   owls _____   10 hounds _____

d Words ending in -gue

Words such as tongue, rogue, catalogue, vague, league, meringue, fatigue, colleague, plague and brogue do not sound the letters ue at the end.

Write the sentences, filling each blank with one of the above words.

1   Another word for language is _____.
2   The black death was a form of bubonic _____.
3   The Football _____ was formed in 1888.
4   A _____ is a list of books or other items.
5   The climbers suffered from extreme _____.

e

1   If you had pencil and paper but could not write, how could you use your materials to convey a message to someone? How accurate would the message be and what would this depend on? Are there any advantages or disadvantages with this form of communication?

2   Explain the essential difference between the sounds made by animals and the language that human beings use.

The beginning of language

How did language begin? We cannot be sure how language began. Nor do we know whether it began in only one part of the world or in several places at once. Equally uncertain is when language began, though it would seem to have developed during the stone age.

One theory about the origin of language is that it began as an imitation of various natural sounds such as the cries of animals, the sound of wind and rain or the breaking of a twig. Other sounds that could be made include human cries of pain, joy, surprise and anger.

Another idea is that the earliest words were sounds that would accompany certain gestures, especially those made by hands and arms. But a person working with the hands would not be able to gesticulate with them. In that case the mouth, lips and tongue might be used to try to copy the hand movements and so begin to form what we call words.

Although we can only guess at how and when language arose, it seems likely that it began because of need. Perhaps when people cooperated in certain ways (in hunting, for example) they would need something more than signs and cries in order to work effectively.

We can also be sure that early language was about the things people did and the tools they used. Having no money, no machinery and no buildings, the people of the stone age and the bronze age would have no words for them.

a   Write a sentence for each answer.

1   How did language begin?
2   When did language begin?
3   Which natural sounds could be imitated by people?
4   Describe another idea about the origin of language.
5   When would a person be unable to signal with the hands?
6   What might be used to try to copy hand movements?
7   Why did language begin?
8   When would people need more than signs and cries?
9   What was early language likely to be about?
10 Why would stone age people have no word for money?

b   Sounds

Write the following, filling each blank with a word to show the sound made.

1   the _____ of a clock
2   the _____ of a drum
3   the _____ of a trumpet
4   the _____ of a cannon
5   the _____ of a siren
6   the _____ of leaves
7   the _____ of corks
8   the _____ of hoofs
9   the _____ of hinges
10 the _____ of bells

c   Write the words from the passage opposite that mean the same as

1   idea or opinion   5   actions
2   beginning   6   signal
3   copy   7   came about
4   go with   8   worked together

d   Sentence construction

Re-write the sentences, beginning each with a word ending with -ing. The last sentence in the passage opposite will show you how.

1   The stone age people had neither cars nor buses and so had no words for them. (**Begin with** Having . . .)
2   I thought that everyone had left, so I switched off the lights. (**Begin with** Thinking . . .)
3   Jill hoped to catch a glimpse of the procession, so she stood on tiptoe. (**Begin with** Hoping . . .)
4   I knew that the shops would be crowded, so I set out in good time. (**Begin with** Knowing . . .)
5   The crew clung to the upturned boat and so managed to avoid drowning. (**Begin with** Clinging . . .)

e

1   About how long ago were the stone age and the bronze age?
2   We know something about the implements used long ago from the relics that have been found. Are we likely to find anything that will help us find out how language began? Give a reason for your answer.

3   Are there any times when people cannot communicate by gesture or sign language – apart from those occasions when the hands and arms are doing something else?

The beginning of writing

The beginning of writing came about through pictures. Pictures can be used to tell a story or to illustrate a particular event or a single object. Thus a picture of the sun would simply mean 'sun'; a picture of an eye would mean 'eye' and so on. Pictures that stand for words are sometimes called pictograms.

The beginning of real writing happened when a picture was used to show an idea and not merely an actual object. In this way a picture of the sun could mean heat or daylight, while a drawing of an eye could mean sight or looking. In time the drawing would become simplified so that a circle would replace a drawing of the sun and would be a symbol or sign rather than a picture. Symbols or signs that represent an idea are called ideograms. Later still, the ideogram for the sun came to be used for the sound 'sun' wherever it appeared.

Picture writing has the advantage that it may enable people who do not know each other's languages to communicate. But some ideas are not easy to set down in pictures, while a complicated message could take a long time to draw. Even then it could be misunderstood by somebody else. A further disadvantage is that this kind of writing tends to become very cumbersome, requiring large numbers of pictures (or characters derived from pictures) to convey a message.

a Write a sentence for each answer.

1 How did the beginning of writing come about?
2 In what ways can pictures be used to convey meaning?
3 What do we call pictures that stand for words?
4 Describe how the beginning of real writing happened.
5 What else (apart from the sun) could a picture of the sun mean?
6 How would the drawing of the sun become simplified?
7 What do we call symbols or signs that represent ideas?
8 What advantage does picture writing have?
9 What disadvantages could there be in setting down a complicated message in pictures?
10 Why do pictograms and ideograms tend to become cumbersome?

b Words ending in -fied

Write the sentences, completing them with words ending in -fied, such as simplified, terrified, electrified, magnified, purified, pacified, defied, amplified, mystified and satisfied.

1 A circle is a _____ drawing of the sun.
2 We were perfectly _____ with the new arrangements.
3 The water was _____ before being used again.
4 The villagers were _____ by the appearance of the lion.
5 The outlaw _____ all attempts to catch him.

c One word for several

Write the sentences, replacing each group of underlined words by one word. Use words taken from the passage opposite.

1 As picture writing developed the drawings were made more simple.
2 A symbol would eventually take the place of a more detailed drawing.
3 A triangle might stand for a tent.
4 People of different races might exchange information and ideas by means of pictures.
5 A disadvantage with pictures is that they can be taken in the wrong sense by other people.

d Words such as project, object, produce, conduct and contract vary their meanings according to how they are said. Write the sentences as shown in no. 1, underlining parts of the words to show where the emphasis lies.

1 Headlands are points of land that proj<u>ect</u> into the sea.
The children were working on a <u>proj</u>ect.
2 A picture can be used to illustrate an object.
Two players began to object to the referee.
3 The farmer was proud of his produce.
I was asked to produce my passport.
4 A baton is used to conduct an orchestra.
They were praised for their good conduct.
5 A hot piece of metal will contract if it is cooled.
The player signed a new contract.

e

1 What ideas and thoughts could lie behind drawings of

a mouth   drums   a lion
a whip   fire   a canoe?

2 Make simplified drawings to represent the following

mountains   a forest   lightning
water   sunrise   fishing.

The first true writing

The first true writing was probably developed by the Sumerians who lived in southern Mesopotamia thousands of years ago. In its earliest form it consisted of ideograms drawn on tablets of wet clay with a stylus made from a reed.

At first the pictures were 'scratched' into the clay, but the stylus picked up a small mound of clay as it went along, so blurring the picture. The Sumerians later discovered that it was easier to make marks by pressing the end of the stylus into the clay. This produced a series of wedge shaped marks, each about 8–9 mm long. The writing, known as cuneiform, gets its name from the shape of the marks, for cuneiform simply means wedge shaped and comes from the Latin word cuneus, meaning a wedge.

The way in which the stylus came to be used meant that it was difficult to make curves and so the earlier picture signs developed into a series of straight marks.

Cuneiform writing is difficult to translate because a character may stand for a word or part of a word. But between about 1800 and 1850 a number of European scholars gradually deciphered an ancient cuneiform inscription, and this enabled people to understand the numerous tablets that had been found. These have provided historians with information that they would not otherwise have had.

a Write a sentence for each answer.

1 Who developed the first true writing?
2 On what did the Sumerians draw their ideograms?
3 What happened when pictures were 'scratched' into the clay?
4 What better method was used to make marks?
5 How long was each mark?
6 What does the word cuneiform mean?
7 Which shapes were the easier to make – curves or straight lines?
8 Why is cuneiform writing difficult to translate?
9 When was cuneiform deciphered?
10 What has our understanding of cuneiform meant to historians?

b Spelling

Write the words to match the definitions. Each one should end with the letters -dge sounding like j.

1 a tapering piece of wood or metal
2 another name for a sleigh
3 a structure carrying a road or railway across a river or road
4 side, rim or boundary; the cutting side of a blade
5 oatmeal cooked in water (or milk)

c Write the words from the passage that mean the same as

1 a pointed instrument used for writing on clay or wax
2 making indistinct
3 change into another language
4 a distinctive mark, letter or sign used in writing
5 little by little; not suddenly
6 worked out the meaning of
7 in any other way

d Write each sentence another way round so as to end with the word underlined.

1 The <u>Sumerians</u> used a system of writing called cuneiform.
2 Cuneiform <u>writing</u> is difficult to translate.
3 Cuneiform <u>writing</u> was used by other people of the ancient world.
4 <u>Sumerian</u> cuneiform is the oldest and the most complicated.
5 In the Sumerian <u>system</u> there were about 600 characters.

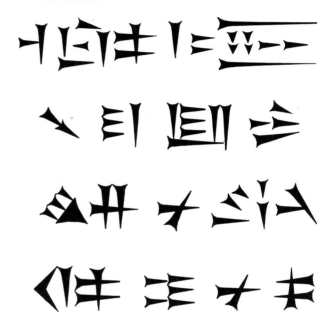

e

1 What would be done to the clay tablets after they had been marked?
2 What is an inscription?
3 To what extent would a stylus be suitable for our kind of writing on paper?
4 Perhaps you do much of your writing with a pencil or ball-pen. Are these writing utensils more suitable for an angular or a cursive style of writing? If you like, copy out a short example of cuneiform to help you decide.

Ancient Egyptian writing

The ancient Egyptians developed a system of writing called hieroglyphics. It consisted of a number of pictures which represented objects, ideas and sounds. The direction of writing is usually from right to left, but sometimes it reads from left to right or even from top to bottom.

Hieroglyphics came into use about 3500–3000 B.C. At first they were used mainly for inscriptions on temples, monuments and tombs. The word hieroglyphics comes from two Greek words meaning sacred carvings because the Greeks thought that only the Egyptian priests understood them.

As knowledge of writing spread the Egyptians needed something more convenient to write on than slabs of stone. So they developed a kind of paper. This was made from layers of the stem of a water plant called papyrus that was then quite plentiful. The layers were pressed together and dried. In order to write on papyrus the scribes used a kind of pen made from a sharpened reed. Ink was made from soot and water.

Hieroglyphic symbols take time to form and so a simplified form of writing called hieratic was worked out. In time this led to an even simpler script called demotic. The word demotic comes from a Greek word meaning the people, which shows that this was the kind of wriing that most Egyptians would then use.

a Write a sentence for each answer.

1   What system of writing did the ancient Egyptians develop?
2   What did ancient Egyptian writing consist of?
3   In which direction are hieroglyphics usually read?
4   When did hieroglyphics come into use?
5   What were hieroglyphics at first used for?
6   What other writing material did the Egyptians develop?
7   What did the scribes use to write with?
8   What was the ink made from?
9   What was the first kind of simplified writing called?
10 What was the later kind of simplified writing called?

b Nouns, verbs, adjectives

Say whether each underlined word is a noun, verb or adjective.

1   A <u>number</u> of ancient civilisations used picture writing.
2   I forgot to <u>number</u> the pages.
3   The <u>stone</u> walls were covered with hieroglyphics.
4   The cottage was built of <u>stone</u>.
5   Papyrus is a <u>plant</u> that grows in the Nile valley.
6   The gardener decided to <u>plant</u> his onion seeds.

c Write the sentences, putting the right parts together.

1   The Egyptian way of writing   were carved on temple walls.
2   Hieroglyphics are an early stage   hieroglyphics were a secret code.
3   Hieroglyphic inscriptions   lasted for thousands of years.
4   By about A.D. 500   until about 1820.
5   People thought that   in the development of writing.
6   Hieroglyphics were not deciphered   knowledge of hieroglyphics had been lost.

d Write out the following as five sentences, putting in all necessary full stops, commas and capital letters.

the rosetta stone was the key to our understanding of hieroglyphics it was a piece of stone measuring 114 × 72cm found near the town of rosetta on the nile delta the stone carried an inscription in three languages hieroglyphics demotic and greek a frenchman called champollion used his knowledge of greek to translate the other two parts champollions work enabled scholars to understand other ancient egyptian writings

e

1   A French Army officer discovered the Rosetta Stone in 1799. What were the French doing in Egypt at that time?
2   Where is the Rosetta Stone now?
3   How do you think we get our word paper?
4   Sumerian and ancient Egyptian are sometimes called dead languages. What is a dead language? Write the names of any other dead languages.

Practice pages

a Compound words beginning with fore-

Write the sentences, completing each with a word beginning with fore-.

1 The _____ supervised the other workpeople.
2 The crew's quarters were in the _____.
3 The tennis champion had a strong _____ stroke.
4 Our _____ are our ancestors.
5 He pointed out the route with his _____.

b Animal sounds

Write the following, filling the blanks with the sounds that the animals make.

1 ducks _____
2 wolves _____
3 cats _____
4 cockerels _____
5 doves _____
6 lambs _____
7 pigs _____
8 turkeys _____
9 mice _____
10 bulls _____

c Words ending in -gue

Write the sentences, filling each blank with a word ending in -gue.

1 A _____ is a type of strong shoe.
2 The _____ absconded with most of the money.
3 A _____ is made from sugar and the white of an egg.
4 The professor and his _____ were working on an experiment.
5 The message was so _____ that nobody knew what it meant.

d Sounds

Write the following, filling each blank with a word to show the sound made.

1 the _____ of a whip
2 the _____ of a bugle
3 the _____ of a bow
4 the _____ of a cane
5 the _____ of a gun
6 the _____ of raindrops
7 the _____ of brakes
8 the _____ of silk
9 the _____ of chains
10 the _____ of feet

e Words ending in -fied

Write the sentences, completing each with a word ending in -fied.

1 The lens _____ the seeds, and we could see the detail clearly.
2 Sound that is _____ is made louder.
3 The parents _____ the distressed children.
4 Some of our railways have been _____.
5 The police were _____ by the man's disappearance.

f Words such as convict, console, subject, record and perfect vary their meanings according to how they are said. Write the sentences as shown in no.1, underlining parts of the words to show where the emphasis lies.

1 It was impossible to con<u>vict</u> the man on such slender evidence.

The <u>con</u>vict climbed over the prison wall.

2 She tried to console the bereaved relatives.

The console sat at the console.

3 The subject of his talk was 'Prehistoric Animals'.

Genghis Khan was able to subject much of central Asia to his rule.

4 Equipment was set up to record the concert.

The athlete set up a new record for the high jump.

5 The lid was a perfect fit.

The inventor was able to perfect his design.

g Nouns, verbs, adjectives

Say whether each underlined word is a noun, verb or adjective.

1 It was a <u>sound</u> idea and everybody supported it.
2 The guard decided to <u>sound</u> the alarm.
3 I listened carefully but couldn't hear a <u>sound</u>.
4 The motorist had to pay a <u>fine</u>.
5 The magistrate had no choice but to <u>fine</u> him.
6 It was a <u>fine</u> day so we went for a walk.
7 A <u>brave</u> person is one who has courage.
8 A North American Indian warrior was sometimes called a <u>brave</u>.
9 The soldiers had to <u>brave</u> the enemy's accurate fire.

h Sentence construction

Rewrite the sentences, beginning each with a word ending with -ing.

1 Amanda burst into the room and told us that she had won. (**Begin with** Bursting . . .)
2 The chairman apologised for the delay and opened the meeting.

3 The driver left his car by the roadside and set out to find help.
4 I pretended that I hadn't seen him and walked away in the opposite direction.
5 We arrived late for the concert and found that all the tickets had been sold.

i How much can you remember?

Write a sentence for each answer.

1 Which came first – written language or spoken language?
2 What is another word for language?
3 What else (apart from eye) could a picture of an eye mean?
4 Where did the Sumerians live?
5 What was Sumerian wedge-shaped writing called?
6 About how many characters were there in the Sumerian system of writing?
7 The ancient Egyptians developed a kind of paper. What was it made from?
8 Where was the Rosetta Stone found?
9 What markings were on the Rosetta Stone?
10 Who deciphered the Rosetta Stone?

j Spelling
Words such as write and writing begin with a silent w. Write the sentences, completing each with a word beginning with a silent w.

1 The _____ was a danger to other ships.
2 The ball struck him on the _____ and broke his watch.
3 The _____ is a small, brown bird.
4 I couldn't see anything _____ with it.
5 The miserable _____ was found sheltering under a hedge.
6 A _____ was placed on the war memorial.
7 The books were _____ in thick brown paper.
8 A _____ is a kind of spanner and is used for turning nuts and bolts.
9 The hand rail was made of _____ iron.
10 The old woman's face was _____ and careworn.

The alphabet

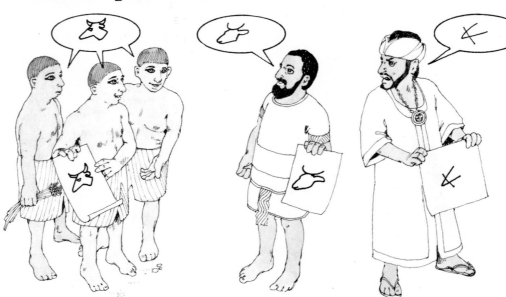

An alphabet is a set of symbols called letters that we use when writing. Each letter stands for a given sound or sounds. Sometimes letters combine to make sounds.

The word alphabet comes from alpha and beta – the names of the first two letters of the Greek alphabet. There are 26 letters in our alphabet – five vowels (a, e, i, o and u) and 21 consonants.

The ancient Egyptians used a pictorial system of writing called hieroglyphics, but this was later simplified so that pictures could indicate syllables as well as words. From this developed a series of signs which may be regarded as the forerunner of a true alphabet.

The Semites, who lived in the Middle East, worked out an alphabetic script that seems to owe something to Egyptian hieroglyphics. One group of Semites, called the Phoenicians, produced a system of 22 signs for the consonants only.

The Greeks traded with the Phoenicians and so got to know about their writing. The Greeks borrowed the Phoenician symbols, altering them to suit their own language. Some Phoenician consonants didn't exist in Greek so the Greeks used the spare signs for the vowels.

The Etruscans, a people living in Italy, knew the Greek alphabet and passed it on to the Romans. The later Roman alphabet had 23 letters and was much like ours. The later addition of J, U and W gave us our 26 letters.

a Write a sentence for each answer.

1   What is an alphabet?
2   What does each letter stand for?
3   How do we get the word alphabet?
4   How many letters are there in our alphabet?
5   Where did the Semites live?
6   What alphabetical system did the Phoenicians produce?
7   How did the Greeks get to know about Phoenician writing?
8   Where did the Etruscans live?
9   How many letters did the later Roman alphabet have?
10 Which letters of our alphabet were added later?

c Alphabetical order

Write these words in alphabetical order, numbering them 1–15.

nomad	laundry	frigate
thermometer	harness	sandal
yacht	jaguar	clarinet
dolphin	quadrant	mosque
answer	woodpecker	violin

d Writing on a page has not always been from left to right. Before this happened there were two earlier stages. Here are three examples to show the three stages in the direction that Greek writing followed.
Read the sentences and then write a paragraph explaining the three stages.

First stage

SIHTEKILNETTIRWEREWSNOITPIRCSNIKEERGYLRAE

Second stage

FONOITCERIDEHTNIEGATSDNOCESEHTSWOHSSIHT
GREEKWRITINGITISSOMETIMESCALLEDPLOUGHWISE
EULCAUOYEVIGSPAHREPYAMESIWHGUOLPDROWEHT

Third stage

THISARRANGEMENTWASUSEDAFTERABOUT500BC

(Spaces between words and the use of small letters came later.)

e

1   How did people preserve such things as stories, poems, traditions etc. before they had any kind of writing?

b Spelling: ph sounding like f

Write out and complete the sentences with words such as phrase, telephone, decipher, elephant, photograph, alphabet, prophesy, graph, pheasant and geography in which the letters ph sound like f.

1   The Greeks used Phoenician symbols in their _____.
2   The _____ is the largest land animal in the world.
3   The doctor examined the _____ of the patient's temperature.
4   We read about other countries in our _____ books.
5   Alexander Graham Bell invented the _____.

2   What else were the Phoenicians noted for besides their alphabet?

Development of the alphabet

We can get some idea of how our letters have come to us by following the development of the letters A, M and R through the ages.

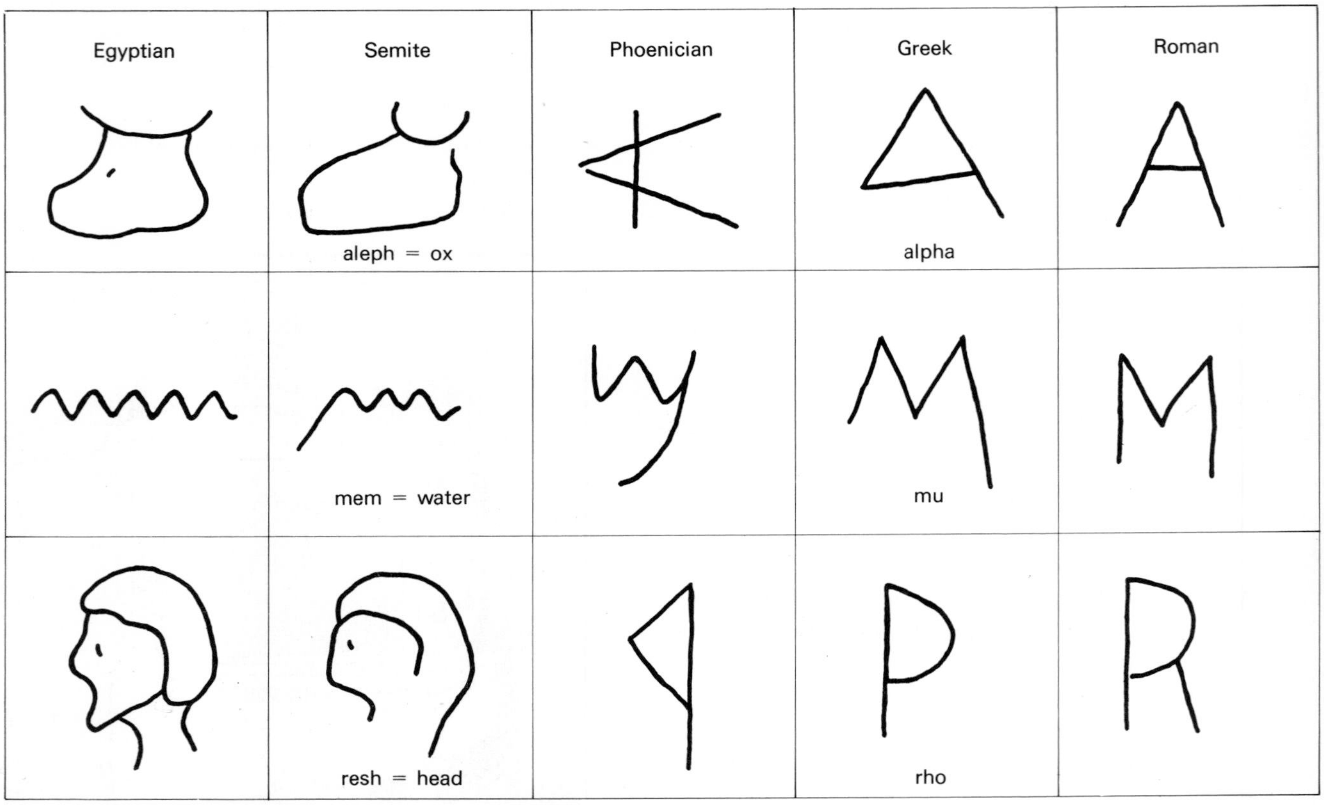

Egyptian	Semite	Phoenician	Greek	Roman
	aleph = ox		alpha	
	mem = water		mu	
	resh = head		rho	

We can trace development of the letter A back to the ancient Egyptian hieroglyphic (pictorial symbol) for an ox. The Semites borrowed and simplified this, called it aleph, which was their word for ox. The third picture shows how the Phoenicians altered the Semite symbol, making it look something like a modern letter A lying on its side. The Greeks adapted the Phoenician letter, calling it alpha. The Roman letter A, shown in the last picture, was derived from the Greek form.

a Write two paragraphs (one for each letter) explaining the origin and development of the letters M and R.

b The alphabet

1 Write the name of the day of the week that begins with the 23rd letter of the alphabet.

2 Write the name of the month of the year that begins with the 6th letter of the alphabet.

3 Which vowel is not used in the word outweigh?

4 Make a word from the letters that come between each of these pairs of letters:

V and X   Q and S   D and F   M and O.

5 Copy out the words in which the letters appear in alphabetical order

first   cloud   ghost   north   chops

c Words derived from Greek

Explain the meanings of the numbered words. The meanings of the Greek words from which they are derived are given.

			Greek	meaning
1	Bible	2 bibliography	biblion	book
3	paternal	4 patriotic	pater	father
5	monopoly	6 monoplane	monos	single
7	geology	8 geography	ge	earth
9	polygon	10 polygamy	polys	many

d Write out the following as six sentences, putting in all necessary capital letters and punctuation marks.

our alphabet has 26 letters but some languages have a different number russian has 33 arabic has 28 gaelic has 18 some alphabets are very complicated and attempts have been made to simplify them in 1928 the turks changed their alphabet from the arabic to the roman style while the japanese have more recently tried to simplify their system of writing

e

1 Here are the names of some of the Greek letters
alpha   omega   gamma   delta   iota   pi.
In what ways do we use these words in English?

2 Here is the inscription over the porch of the Pantheon, a Roman temple completed in A.D. 126. What do you notice about the style of the lettering?

M AGRIPPA L F COS TERTIVM FECIT

The Roman alphabet

The Romans took their alphabet from the Etruscans, who got it from the Greeks, altering the shapes of some letters and adding one or two more of their own.

At first the Roman alphabet consisted of capital letters only. The style of lettering was graceful, clear and easy to read from a distance. This was especially important when the lettering was some way above ground, as in inscriptions on buildings, arches and memorial columns.

The carving of letters on stone led to an interesting development. The carvers found that it was the unconnected ends of letters that caused most problems. No matter how carefully they worked, the carvers found it difficult to make the ends look neat so they finished them off with a short cross-line. These short cross-lines are called serifs. The Romans also varied the thickness of the strokes they used in lettering. Both these features are still in use in many printing styles of to-day.

Roman children learnt their letters by writing them on wooden tablets coated with wax. They wrote with a pointed instrument called a stylus. The wax never hardened and any mistakes were therefore easy to correct. This also meant that, when a piece of work was finished with, the wax could be made smooth again so that more writing could be done.

For more permanent records the Romans used papyrus or (more commonly) parchment.

a Write a sentence for each answer.

1 From whom did the Romans take their alphabet?
2 Describe Roman lettering.
3 When was it especially important for the lettering to be clear?
4 Which parts of letters caused the carvers most problems?
5 How were the unconnected ends of letters finished off?
6 What are the short cross-lines called?
7 How did Roman children learn their letters?
8 What writing instrument did the children use?
9 Explain why the wax tablets could be used more than once.
10 What else did the Romans write on?

b Adjectives and adverbs

Notice the spelling of the adjective graceful (line 5) and the adverb carefully (line 12) and the way in which these words are used.

Write the sentences, completing each with an adjective or adverb formed from the word on the left.

care   1 He walked _____ across the icy road.

success 2 We were _____ at the second attempt.

beauty   3 The mural was _____ painted.

grace   4 She danced _____ round the stage.

respect 5 The crew were _____ to their captain.

thank   6 I was _____ to see him safe and well.

c Words derived from Latin

Latin was the language of the Roman Empire and many of our words are of Latin origin.

Explain the meanings of the numbered words. The meanings of the Latin words from which they are derived are given.

				Latin	meaning
1	centurion	2	century	centum	one hundred
3	supervise	4	superior	super	above, over
5	manuscript	6	manual	manus	hand
7	multitude	8	multiple	multus	many
9	union	10	unison	unus	one

d Write out the following as five sentences, putting in all necessary capital letters and punctuation marks.

papyrus was the monopoly of the egyptians and they either charged other people dearly for it or prohibited its export altogether so other people began to look for an alternative and this led to the discovery of parchment this took place in pergamum a greek city in asia minor in about 190 b c parchment is made from the skins of animals such as sheep or goats a fine quality parchment called vellum is made from the skins of young animals such as calves lambs or kids

e

1 Write out the Latin words that these abbreviations stand for and say what they mean in English.

A.D.   a.m.   p.m.   etc.   N.B.

Write any other abbreviations that stand for Latin words.

2 Parchment was so strong that anything written on it could be rubbed off. Why do you think this was done? What harm might be done by this action?

The English language

Nowadays English is spoken in many parts of the world, but there was really no such thing as the English language before about A.D. 450. Up till then the people in Britain spoke a Celtic dialect. The Romans occupied Britain from A.D. 43 to about A.D. 410 but their language made little impression on the native population.

Soon after the Romans left Britain the Anglo-Saxon occupation began. This was a gradual settlement rather than a sudden invasion and went on until about the year 700.

The Anglo-Saxons were Germanic tribes and their language became the dominant one in their new home. This form of English, as it came to be known, is often called Old English, although to us now it looks like a foreign language.

In the years 750–1050 there were a number of raids carried out by the Vikings, and we can trace Viking influence on place names and other words that passed into our language.

The last invasion of Britain was in 1066. This time the invaders were the Normans, who came from France. The conquerors spoke French, but ordinary folk continued to speak English, and by about 1400 this had become the language that most people in Britain used. By now, English had absorbed numerous French words, many of which are of Latin origin.

The English that was used about 500 years ago is sometimes called Middle English, and even this looks strange to us now. Many more changes were to take place before it became the language that we know to-day.

a Write a sentence for each answer.

1 What language did the people of Britain speak before about A.D. 450?
2 What effect on the language of Britain did the Roman occupation have?
3 When did the Anglo-Saxon occupation of Britain begin?
4 Which language became the dominant one in England?
5 What happened in about 750–1050 to bring new words into English?
6 Who invaded Britain in 1066?
7 What language did the conquerors speak?
8 Which language had become widely used in Britain by about 1400?
9 What was the origin of many of the French words?
10 What name is given to the English used about 500 years ago?

b Words ending in -er and -or

Write the words to match these definitions.

1 A person who conquers.
2 A person who competes.
3 A person who explores.
4 A dealer in jewels.
5 A person who invents.
6 A person who writes.
7 A person who acts.
8 A person who employs others.
9 A person who manufactures.
10 A person who collects.

c Passed and past

Write the sentences, completing each with either passed or past.

1 Many foreign words have _____ into our language.
2 It has been very wet during the _____ week.
3 Mandy _____ her driving test yesterday.
4 The programme began at half _____ two.
5 The week's holiday _____ quickly.
6 Mark _____ the ball to his goalkeeper.
7 He talked a lot about his _____ life.
8 The dog wouldn't let us get _____.

d Here are two short specimens of language for you to translate into modern English.

The first, in Old English, is the beginning of a prayer. (The strange-looking letter þ is called thorn and makes the sound th.)

The second specimen, in Middle English, is from the Wycliffe Bible of 1389.

1 Faeder ure, þu þe eart in heofonum, si þin nama gehalgod.
2 Forsothe when Jhesus hadde comen doun fro the hil, many cumpanyes folewiden hym.

e

1 Explain how we get the words England and English.
2 The Normans came from Normandy which is in France. Explain the origins of the words Norman and Normandy.
3 Where did the Vikings come from?

Printing

Printing is one of the most important means of communication. Without it you would not now be reading this book. Even the development of radio and television has not diminished the importance of printing.

The first printing was done from wood blocks, the shapes of the letters being carved by hand. But this was a slow process, requiring much skill and patience, and every page of every book had to be carved separately.

A great step forward was the use of movable type. The Chinese discovered this in the 11th century, but it was not known in Europe until about 1440. In this method of printing individual letters were made from separate pieces of metal. These letters could be assembled to make words and sentences. If the letters were inked over and pressed on to paper they would print the words. When the printing was finished the letters could be taken apart and re-arranged to print something else.

One of the first European books to be printed in movable type was Johann Gutenberg's 42-line Bible. (It had 42 lines on each page.)

The first book to be printed in English was one that recounted the history of Troy. It was printed in Flanders in 1474 by an Englishman, William Caxton. In 1476 he returned to England and established a printing press at Westminster. Altogether he printed nearly 80 books, many being his own translations from the French.

a Write a sentence for each answer.

1 How was the first printing done?
2 What were the disadvantages of printing from wood blocks?
3 Who discovered the use of movable type?
4 When was the use of movable type known in Europe?
5 Describe the method of printing by movable type.
6 Who printed the 42-line Bible?
7 How did the 42-line Bible get its name?
8 What was the first book printed in English about?
9 Where did Caxton set up a printing press in England?
10 How many books did Caxton print?

b Write words to match the definitions. Each answer begins with the letters tele-, from the Greek meaning 'at a distance' or 'far'.

1 a means of sending and receiving pictures by electronic signals
2 a device that enables us to speak to people at a distance
3 an instrument for looking at distant objects
4 a message sent by telegraph
5 a way of sending and receiving thoughts without speaking, writing or making any kind of sign or signal

c Write the words from the passage opposite that mean the same as

1 lessened   3 one at a time   5 gave an account of
2 needing   4 put together   6 set up

d Write the following as five sentences, putting in all necessary capital letters and punctuation marks.

most historians consider johann gutenberg to be the inventor of movable type in europe although a dutch printer called laurens coster had been working on the same idea at first gutenberg worked in secret this may have been to keep the idea to himself or he may have felt that some people would mistrust his invention even when printing had been established some people regarded it as a kind of magic or 'black art' they could not understand why all printed copies of a book looked alike and how they could be made so quickly

e

1 How were books produced before any kind of printing had been invented?
2 Where is Flanders?
3 Make a list of items (such as books, newspapers, catalogues) that are printed.
4 What other material had to be made in quantity before books could be produced on a large scale?

Practice pages

a Spelling

Write the words to match the definitions. Each one should end with the letters -dge sounding like j.

1 A person in charge of a court of law.
2 A sign or emblem to show membership or position.
3 A row of bushes or low trees forming a fence.
4 To move quickly to one side to avoid something or someone.
5 To give a slight push, usually with the elbow.

b Alphabetical order

Write these words in alphabetical order, numbering them 1–15.

imitation	guard	pyramid
equator	elephant	biscuit
bottle	aircraft	illustration
kitchen	knight	professional
puppet	gnome	alligator

c Words derived from Greek

Explain the meanings of the numbered words. The meanings of the Greek words from which they are derived are given.

				Greek	meaning
1	pentathlon	2	pentagon	pente	five
3	astronomy	4	astronaut	astron	star
5	megaphone	6	megatherium	megas	great
7	hydrofoil	8	hydrant	hydor	water
9	microfilm	10	microbe	mikros	small

d Adjectives and adverbs

Write the sentences, completing each with either an adjective (as in no. 1) or an adverb (as in no. 2) formed from the word on the left.

faith	1	The old dog was <u>faithful</u> to its master.
pain	2	I was <u>painfully</u> aware that my ankle was sore.
wrong	3	The man was _____ accused of fraud.
wonder	4	The acrobats gave a _____ display of their skills.
cheer	5	They waited _____ for the match to begin.
hope	6	We were _____ that the weather would improve.
colour	7	The art exhibition was very _____.
taste	8	Everything was _____ arranged.
joy	9	News of the victory was _____ received.
harm	10	Overeating can be _____.

e Spelling: ph sounding like f

Write out and complete the sentences with words in which the letters ph sound like f.

1 A _____ is a short group of words.

2 The _____ is a game bird with a long tail.

3 A _____ is a picture produced by a camera.

4 To _____ means to foretell what will happen.

5 For years no one knew how to _____ hieroglyphics.

6 Write the letters that follow each of these letters in alphabetical order: D, L, T.

7 Write the next letter in this series: F, H, J, L.

8 Which vowel does not appear in the word PROVIDENTIAL?

9 Which letter occurs once in APPLE, twice in PLENTIFUL and three times in PARALLEL?

10 Write out and complete the analogy: B is to G as N is to _____.

f Words derived from Latin

Explain the meanings of the numbered words. The meanings of the Latin words from which they are derived are given.

		Latin	meaning
1 aquarium	2 aqueduct	aqua	water
3 bicycle	4 biplane	bi	twice
5 omnibus	6 omnipotent	omnis	all
7 pedal	8 pedestrian	pes	foot
9 contraband	10 contradict	contra	against

g Words ending in -er and -or

Write the words to match the definitions.

1 A person who commands.
2 A person who inspects.
3 A person who directs.
4 A person who defends.
5 A person who sails.
6 A person who governs.
7 A person who lectures.
8 A person who announces.
9 A person who gives blood.
10 A person who studies the stars.

h The alphabet

1 Which letter comes between R and T?

2 Make two words out of these letters of the alphabet: 1st, 3rd, 5th, 12th and 19th.

3 Which letter is used most often in the word MULTIMILLIONAIRE?

4 Which letter is used once only in the word REMEMBER?

5 Which letter occurs in REGISTER but not in RESIST?

English as a world language

It is perhaps unfortunate that there is no single language that everyone in the world understands. At the moment the nearest thing to a universal language is English.

Nevertheless, it is obviously useful if people from different countries can use the same language when dealing with certain matters. The pictures that follow suggest a number of situations where the same language is being used each time. Sometimes the countries of the world have made an agreement about this so as to avoid confusion. In other cases it is simply convenient to use English because so many people all over the world can understand it.

a Explain what is happening in each picture, pointing out how it can be an advantage to use one language and where there has been argeement to do so.

b Occupations

Name the occupations of the people described here. Explain how it could be helpful to each of these people if there were such a thing as a world language.

1 Someone who looks after the needs of passengers on air-liners.

2 A person who controls a game by seeing that the rules are obeyed.

3 Someone who accompanies a group of tourists on conducted tours.

4 A person engaged in commerce, buying and selling goods on a large scale.

5 Someone who first meets or receives guests at a hotel.

6 A person engaged in running affairs between the government of one country and that of another.

c Here are five sentences about artificial languages, but they are in the wrong order. Write them in the correct order.

It was followed a few years later by Esperanto. This has become the most successful artificial language.
Over the years several artificial languages have been created.
Unfortunately, Volapuk was very complicated and soon died out.
The first one, called Volapuk, was created in 1879.

d Write out the following as five sentences, putting in all necessary capital letters and punctuation marks.

another attempt to devise a world language was called basic english it was devised by c k ogden and i a richards between 1925 and 1932 the idea was to produce a kind of simplified english that would be easy for everyone to learn altogether there are about 600000 english words but basic english used only about 800 of these a number of books were translated into basic english but in recent years the idea has not been widely used

e

1 Suggest reasons why English is used in so many parts of the world.

2 Identify this language from the clues given. It is spoken by more people than is any other language – over 800 million people. In its spoken form there are many different dialects. It has no alphabet, but uses more than 40,000 characters.

How suitable – or unsuitable – would this language be as a world language? Give reasons for your answer.

How we get new words

Any living language is constantly changing. New words are needed from time to time, while others are discarded or forgotten. How many of us know the meanings of mickle, trow or maugre? What is a paynim? What about eft, eme and enow? And what would people of long ago make of astronaut, blackout, tachograph and disco?

Why does language change? Language changes because it needs new words for new inventions, discoveries, instruments and ideas. Words sometimes drop out of use because they are names of things that people no longer use.

Where do new words come from? Sometimes an invention takes on the name of the inventor, or a material may be called after the place where it was first made. Many new words come from Latin or Greek. Some, like focus (Latin) and thorax (Greek) are taken bodily from these languages, but more often new words are made up out of Latin and Greek parts. The word multinational comes from two Latin words; protoplasm comes from two Greek. Sometimes (as in automobile and television) there is a mixture of Latin and Greek.

In some instances – as with knave, villain and silly – we keep old words and give them new meanings. We realise that this process is still going on when we consider such words as square, liquidate, capsule and module. Sometimes – as with fabulous, chronic and allergic – a new and popular meaning almost obliterates the old.

a Write a sentence for each answer.

1 Why does language change?
2 Why do words sometimes drop out of use?
3 How are inventions sometimes named?
4 How are materials sometimes named?
5 From which old languages do many new words come?
6 From which language do we get the word multinational?
7 From which language do we get the word protoplasm?
8 From which languages do we get the word automobile?
9. From which languages do we get the word television?
10 What has happened to the meaning of words such as fabulous and chronic?

b Making new words

One way of making new words is to join two existing words.

Add a word to the first word in each line to make a new word that will match the definition.

1 run_____   A strip of land where planes land or take off.
2 under_____   A road that passes under another road.
3 sun_____   A darker patch on the sun's surface.
4 space_____   A vehicle for interplanetary travel.
5 black_____   A period without artificial lights or the deliberate concealment of all lights.

6–10 Now write five sentences, using the words you have written for nos. 1–5.

c Acronyms

Acronyms are words formed mainly from the initial letters of other words.

Write the acronyms made from these words:

1 North Atlantic Treaty Organisation
2 Defence of the Realm Act
3 Radio detection and ranging apparatus
4 National Association of Local Government Officers
5 Electronic random number indicator equipment
6 Light Amplification by the stimulated emission of radiation

d Some materials and items of clothing are called after the names of places.

Say what each item is and give the name of the place (e.g. town, island, country) from which it gets its name.

1 Balaclava   6   Cashmere
2 Jersey   7   Denim
3 Bikini   8   Calico
4 Fez   9   Suede
5 Duffel   10 Muslin

e

1 A word on page 28 comes from two Greek words meaning 'star sailor'. Write the word.
2 Pandemonium, chortle and runcible are words invented by writers. Find out what the words mean and who invented them.
3 To whom do these trade names belong and how were they formed?
   QANTAS SABENA FIAT SAAB

Borrowed words

As well as drawing on Latin and Greek, English has borrowed many words from languages throughout the world. This has come about partly because of the growth in world-wide trade and travel and partly as a result of Britain's share in exploration, discovery and colonisation. Many of these loan words are now part of our everyday speech and we are hardly conscious of using foreign words.

a Make a list of the items illustrated above, numbering them 1 to 9. Alongside each write the name of the part of the world where the word comes from, choosing your answers from this list: Australia, Czechoslovakia, Holland, Italy, Spain, Persia, Malaya, Africa and India.

b All the words in each list are taken from the same language and all are connected with the same subject. In each case, give the name of the language and say what the words are about.

1 buffet, casserole, consommé, croquette, gateau, hors d'oeuvre, pâte, purée, rotisserie, soufflé.

2 allegro, andante, aria, cantabile, concerto, crescendo, intermezzo, largo, pizzicato, staccato.

c Plurals

Write the plurals of these words.

1	kangaroo	5	igloo	9	tattoo
2	piano	6	casino	10	salvo
3	chef	7	scarf	11	potato
4	bureau	8	plateau	12	tomato

d Write the following list of words and where they come from, re-arranging the words in column B in the correct order.

	A	B
1	fiord	France
2	chimpanzee	New Zealand (Maori word)
3	boomerang	Italy
4	café	Norway
5	waltz	Spain
6	piccolo	Australia
7	judo	North America (Indian word)
8	kiwi	Africa
9	tomahawk	Germany
10	vanilla	Japan

e

1 Who are the Maoris?

2 Some borrowed words change their spelling when they are used in another language. Write the English words that come from these German words.

kobalt   quarz   pudel

3 Find out the origin of these words.

algebra	balsa	geyser
broccoli	kiosk	shampoo
tattoo	toboggan	umbrella
mosquito	oasis	sauna
skipper	ukulele	kimono

$$\frac{mv^2}{a} = mv\omega = ma\omega^2 = \frac{Ze^2}{a^2} \quad\text{—} \quad ①$$

$$P = \frac{nh}{2\pi} = mva = ma\omega^2 \quad\text{—}② $$

where n is an integer.

Dividing ① by ② :

$$v = a\omega = \frac{2\pi Ze^2}{nh}$$

$$\Rightarrow a = \frac{n^2 h^2}{4\pi^2 m Ze^2} \; ; \; \omega = \frac{8\pi^3 m Z^2 e^4}{n^3 h^3} \; ;$$

$$\Upsilon = \frac{2\pi}{\omega} = \frac{n^3 h^3}{4\pi^2 m Z^2 e^4} .$$

$$E_{tot} = E_{kin} + E_{pot}$$

$$E_{kin} = \frac{1}{2} mv^2 = \frac{2\pi^2 m Z^2 e^4}{n^2 h^2}$$

$$E_{pot} = -\frac{Ze^2}{a} = \frac{-4\pi^2 m Z^2 e^4}{n^2 h^2}$$

$$\text{Thus } E_{tot} = \frac{-2\pi^2 m Z e^4}{h^2} \cdot \frac{1}{n^2}$$

The Bohr Model of a Hydrogen Atom

Spelling

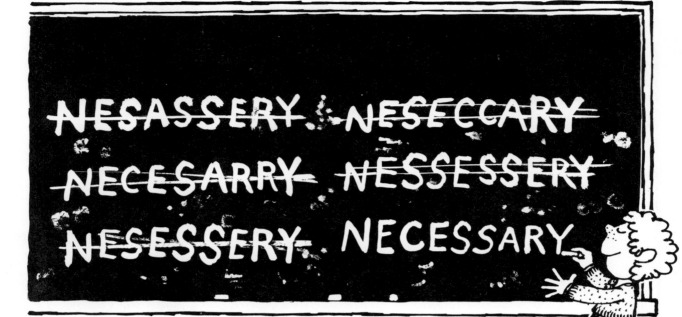

A problem that many of us face from time to time is how to spell a word. The chief cause of spelling difficulty is that spelling and pronunciation (how we say words) don't always match very well. We can show this by spelling fish as 'ghoti', taking the 'gh' from cough to give the f sound, the 'o' from women to give the i sound and the 'ti' from nation to give the sh sound. The letter 'e' appears three times in 'defender' but each time it makes a different sound. What about vase and case, both and moth, work and fork? Why do we have so many problems?

One reason is that some words used to be pronounced differently. Pairs such as sea and see, feet and feat didn't always sound alike. We probably don't make any distinction between the way we say father and farther, but it is likely that the first 'r' in farther used to be given a distinctive trill. As pronunciations change we are left with spellings that may confuse us.

A common spelling difficulty concerns silent letters. Why do we have a 'b' in subtle and a 'p' in receipt? Such a problem often comes about through the origins of a word. Subtle comes from sub tela and receipt from recipere – both Latin. Perhaps our spelling would be easier without these 'extra' letters, but some people think that, for example, we should keep the 'b' in debt (from the Latin debitum) to show where the word came from.

a Write a sentence for each answer.

1 What is the chief cause of spelling difficulty?
2 What is meant by pronunciation?
3 Explain how we can spell 'fish' as 'ghoti'?
4 What is remarkable about the pronunciation of the letter 'e' in defender?
5 What distinction used to be made between the pronunciation of father and farther?
6 Which letter is silent in subtle?
7 Which letter is silent in receipt?
8 Where does the word subtle come from?
9 Where does the word receipt come from?
10 How do we get the word debt?

b A letter has been missed out of each of these words. Write the words as they should be.

1	adress	6	carrige	11	imediately
2	curant	7	exitement	12	forman
3	anser	8	Febuary	13	garantee
4	choclate	9	parliment	14	medcine
5	squirel	10	gide	15	apetite

c A letter has been added to each of these words. Write the words as they should be.

1	daffodill	6	tradgedy	11	quarrell
2	traffick	7	luggagge	12	ammount
3	rabbitt	8	annuall	13	icickle
4	fourty	9	wallnut	14	priviledge
5	gorrilla	10	untill	15	ashphalt

d Here are some words that have been spelt as they sound. Write the words as they should be.

1	sed	6	plow	11	senter
2	frend	7	dokter	12	bom
3	skool	8	hoo	13	nok
4	rong	9	gost	14	laf
5	kof	10	ake	15	bort

e

1 Write the sentences, choosing the correct words from those in brackets.

a We bought some (stationary, stationery) from the newsagent.
b She used to (practice, practise) the piano every day.
c If you have a television set you have to have a (licence, license).
d He wouldn't accept (advice, advise) from anyone.
e The shoes were not (quiet, quite) what I wanted.

2 Some people have suggested that our spelling should be simplified so that words would be spelt as they are pronounced. If this were done, what advantages and disadvantages would there be?

Overworked words

We have seen that the English language has drawn words from many other languages. This gives us a great variety of words and expressions to use and so we do not need to go on repeating the same ones over and over again. Some familiar words have been so well-used that perhaps they are due for a rest.

Words such as got, nice, put, good, some, big and little are so easy to use that we sometimes forget that there are many others that could be used instead. Not only do the alternatives make an agreeable change – they can often express more precisely what we are trying to say.

a Re-write each of these sentences without using the word got. Make any other detailed changes in the wording that you consider necessary, but do not alter the meaning.

1 We got on the train at Manchester.
2 The continual noise got on my nerves.
3 They have got on well since they enlarged the shop.
4 The battalion got out while there was still the chance to do so.
5 The bus company got out a new time table.
6 Eventually we got over the shock.
7 For a time the patient's condition got worse.
8 After a few days his health got better.
9 Jane got full marks for her work.
10 He got through his final examination without difficulty.
11 The prisoners got away by climbing a high wall.
12 I got round Father to take me to the match.

b Re-write these phrases, substituting other words in place of nice. Use a different word each time. Change a to an where necessary.

1 a nice day
2 a nice fire
3 a nice smell
4 a nice garden
5 a nice drink
6 a nice argument
7 a nice girl
8 a nice mess
9 a nice thought
10 a nice orange
11 a nice dog
12 a nice present

c Re-write each of these sentences without using the word put. Make any other detailed changes in the wording that you consider necessary, but do not alter the meaning.

1 He decided to put in for the job.
2 The ship put about because of bad weather.
3 I put the milk into the jug.
4 The old lady was hard put to it to pay the rent.
5 The property was put up for sale.
6 We were able to put them up for the night.
7 The author was put out by the bad reviews of his book.
8 All the mistakes were put right.
9 We put the bulbs in the front garden.
10 Although Tim was small he would not let the bigger boys put on him.
11 The programme was put out at eight o'clock.
12 The lights were put out at ten o'clock each evening.

d Re-write these phrases, substituting other words in place of good. Use a different word each time. Change a to an where necessary.

1 a good boy
2 a good look
3 a good book
4 a good joke
5 a good light
6 a good worker
7 a good holiday
8 a good dinner
9 a good idea
10 a good driver
11 a good dancer
12 a good match

e

1 Re-write each of these sentences without using the word some. Use different words each time.

a I try to save some money each week.
b We saw some soldiers marching along the road.
c There was some milk left in the jug.
d There were some cars in the car park.
e In spite of the cool breeze, some people were bathing in the sea.
f We were kept waiting for quite some time.

2 Make a list of words that could be used instead of big. Here are a few incomplete words to help you. Add as many others as you can.

ext _ _ _ _ _ e   enorm _ _ _

v _ _ t   gig _ _ _ _ _

h _ _ e   col _ _ _ _ _

b _ _ ky   imm _ _ _ _

mass _ _ _   tre _ _ _ _ ous

Practice pages

a Write the following list of words and the places where they come from, re-arranging the words in column B in the correct order.

	A	B
1	budgerigar	China
2	ballet	Malaya
3	kindergarten	Eskimo
4	gondola	Spain
5	orang-utan	France
6	squaw	Russia
7	igloo	Italy
8	armada	Australia
9	tea	North America (Indian word)
10	vodka	Germany

b Making new words

Add a word to the first word in each line to make a new word that will match the definition.

1 under_____ The landing gear of an aircraft.

2 skate_____ A short strip of wood mounted on small wheels.

3 air_____ Emergency transport of supplies by aircraft.

4 soap_____ Small, thin pieces of soap for washing clothes.

5 lay_____ A small parking area at the side of a road.

6 task_____ An armed force formed for a special purpose.

7 moon_____ The physical appearance of the moon's surface.

8 hatch_____ The rear, upward-opening door of a car.

9 motor_____ A fast road with no roundabouts, crossroads etc.

10 man_____ Men (or people) available for work or military service.

11 splash_____ The landing of a spacecraft in the sea.

12 stock_____ A reserve supply of materials or arms.

13 flash_____ A scene in a film showing an earlier event.

14 news_____ Paper on which newspapers are printed.

15 out_____ The amount or number of things produced or made.

16 cut_____ A reduction.

17 score_____ A screen or hoarding showing the score in a game.

18 wind_____ A passage in which such things as aircraft are tested.

c A letter has been missed out of each of these words. Write the words as they should be.

1	aquaintance	9	ryme
2	hansome	10	posess
3	musle	11	necesary
4	letuce	12	miniture
5	artic	13	shedule
6	neumonia	14	lepard
7	juce	15	reumatism
8	colum	16	qickly

d A letter has been added to each of these words. Write the words as they should be.

1	unneccessary	9	harrass
2	accurrate	10	ommitted
3	coacoa	11	occassion
4	vigourous	12	garrisson
5	proffessor	13	playgue
6	tresspassers	14	blissfull
7	longtitude	15	fullfil
8	parraffin	16	aggreggate

e Here are some words that have been spelt as they sound. Write the words as they should be.

1	biskit	9	sosij
2	eko	10	opake
3	bild	11	perswade
4	nashun	12	zilafone
5	det	13	fotograf
6	parashoot	14	silinder
7	skeme	15	sarm
8	dorter	16	enuf

f Write the sentences, filling the blanks in each pair with words of similar sound but different meaning and spelling.

1 Sightseers were kept away from the _____ of the crash.

2 I had _____ the programme before.

3 Vegetarians do not eat _____.

4 We arranged to _____ again on the following Wednesday.

5 Some of the _____ fluid had leaked.

6 There was a _____ for coffee at half past ten.

7 The ice _____ was drifting towards the ship.

8 We could do nothing to stem the _____ of water.

9 The umpire replaced the dislodged _____.

10 The straw was arranged in neat _____.

g Make a list of words that could be used instead of little. Here are a few incomplete words to help you. Add as many others as you can.

infinit _ _ _ _ _l	dim _ _ _ tive
li _ _ ted	tri _ _ _ l
p _ _ y	micro _ _ _ _ _ _
trif _ _ _ _	b _ _ _ f
pa _ _ _ y	f _ _ e

h How much can you remember?

Write a sentence for each answer.

1 What do we call letters that are not vowels?

2 How many letters has the Russian alphabet?

3 How many letters has the Gaelic alphabet?

4 What changes did the Turks make to their alphabet in 1928?

5 Where did the discovery of parchment take place?

6 What is parchment made from?

7 What is vellum?

8 Who is considered to be the inventor of movable type in Europe?

9 At first Gutenberg worked in secret. Why was this?

10 What are Volapuk and Esperanto?

i Nouns, verbs, adjectives

Say whether each underlined word is a noun, verb or adjective.

1 The driver was a <u>key</u> witness.

2 She kept the <u>key</u> in her purse.

3 We have a Venetian <u>blind</u> in the kitchen.

4 The <u>blind</u> man carried a white stick.

5 It was time for the passengers to <u>board</u> the plane.

6 Several notices were pinned to the <u>board</u>.

7 I <u>saw</u> her at the concert last night.

8 The old <u>saw</u> was rather rusty.

9 The <u>cold</u> weather kept people indoors.

10 My sister has a bad <u>cold</u>.

11 One <u>piece</u> of the jig-saw puzzle was missing.

12 She tried to <u>piece</u> the fragments together.

13 Mrs Black had to <u>badger</u> her husband to cut the grass.

14 The <u>badger</u> is a nocturnal, burrowing mammal.

15 The new school has a <u>flat</u> roof.

16 My auntie lives in a <u>flat</u>.

Days of the week

Among Christian peoples Sunday is the first day of the week and a day often reserved for rest and worship. The name comes from two Old English words 'sunnan daeg', meaning sun's day. Among pagan peoples the day was regarded as being sacred to the sun. The early Christians had to work on Sunday, but by about 300 the day was acknowledged as a day of rest.

Monday takes its name from the Old English 'monan daeg', meaning moon's day. In olden times Monday was held to be sacred to the goddess of the moon.

The third day of the week is named after Tyr, the old Norse god of war. His name is sometimes spelt Tiu or Tiw, giving the Old English 'Tiwes daeg', from which we get our Tuesday.

Wednesday gets its name from 'Wodnes daeg', which is Old English for Woden's day. Woden (or Wotan) is the Germanic form of the Norse god Odin.

One of Odin's sons was Thor, the Norse god of thunder. From him we get our word Thursday. The Anglo-Saxon god Thunor or Thunar and the German Donar are akin to Thor.

The Old English word 'Frigedaeg', meaning Frigg's day, gives us the word Friday for the sixth day of the week. Frigg or Frigga was the wife of Odin in Norse mythology.

Saturday is Saturn's day (Old English Saeter-daeg) and is called after the Roman god of agriculture.

a Write a sentence for each answer.

1 Among which people is Sunday the first day of the week?
2 How do we get the word Sunday?
3 How do we get the word Monday?
4 How do we get the name Tuesday?
5 How does Wednesday get its name?
6 What is the Norse name for Woden or Wotan?
7 From which of Odin's sons do we get the word Thursday?
8 Which day of the week is Frigga's day?
9 Who was Frigga's husband?
10 How do we get the word Saturday?

b To show possession the apostrophe is placed at the end of the word. For example:

The girl's coats = The coats of the girl (one girl)
The girls' coats = The coats of the girls (more than one girl).

Write the numbered sentences, putting in apostrophes to show possession.

The home of the Norse gods was called Asgard.
1 The Norse gods home was called Asgard.
The spear of Odin was made by the dwarfs.
2 Odins spear was made by the dwarfs.
Odin made plans to meet the threat of the giants.
3 Odin made plans to meet the giants threat.
The hall of the warriors was called Valhalla.
4 The warriors hall was called Valhalla.
The wounds of the warriors were made whole.
5 The warriors wounds were made whole.
One of the giants stole the hammer of Thor.
6 One of the giants stole Thors hammer.

c Write the words from the passage opposite that mean the same as

1 set apart   3 thought of   5 related
2 heathen   4 recognised   6 farming

d Write the sentences, filling each blank with an adjective connected with, or derived from, the god or goddess whose name is in brackets. (The adjectives should have small letters.)

1 A _____ (Jove) person is merry and full of fun.
2 The _____ (Flora) decorations were very colourful.
3 The weight lifter was a man of _____ (Hercules) strength.
4 The regimental band played a selection of _____ (Mars) music.
5 A _____ (Mercury) person is quick and sprightly.

e

1 The Romans named their days after the sun, the moon and five planets – Mars, Mercury, Jupiter, Venus and Saturn. Why didn't they use the names of the planets Uranus, Neptune and Pluto?
2 What is meant by the Sabbath?
3 When do these days occur?
Shrove Tuesday   Ash Wednesday   Good Friday
What is their special meaning and importance?

Months of the year

All our names for the months of the year are based on the Roman. The earliest Roman calendar that we know of consisted of ten months called Martius, Aprilis, Maius, Junius, Quintilis, Sextilis, September, October, November and December. Januarius and Februarius were added later – but at the end of the year.

Like other ancient calendars the Roman was not very accurate, the problem being that it did not keep in step with the seasons. To make up the difference the Romans added extra days every other year, but this was not very satisfactory.

By 46 B.C. the calendar was about three months ahead of where it should have been, so Julius Caesar asked an Alexandrian astronomer called Sosigenes to help. The result was a calendar of 12 months, beginning with January. Every fourth year would be a leap year. Later, Quintilis was renamed July (in honour of Julius Caesar) and Sextilus was changed to August (after the emperor Augustus).

The Julian calendar was a big improvement, but each year was about 11 minutes too long. This may not seem much, but by the year 1580 the discrepancy amounted to 10 days. So the Pope (Gregory XIII) decreed that 10 days be removed from the calendar and that, from then on, only the century years that could be divided exactly by 400 would be leap years.

Britain did not adopt the Gregorian calendar until 1752, by which time it was necessary to shorten the year by 11 days.

a Write a sentence for each answer.

1 How do we get our names for the months of the year?

2 How many months were there in the earliest known Roman calendar?

3 How far wrong was the Roman calendar by 46 B.C.?

4 Whom did Julius Caesar consult and what was the result?

5 How was Quintilis later renamed?

6 How was Sextilus later renamed?

7 How inaccurate was the Julian calendar?

8 How big had the discrepancy become by 1580?

9 What changes in the calendar did Pope Gregory decree?

10 When did Britain adopt the Gregorian calendar?

b Using the information given, write sentences telling how we get the names of these months.

1 January – Roman god Janus – Janus had two faces looking opposite ways, one to past, one to future.
   (You could begin with the words 'January is named after . . .' or 'We get our word January . . .')

2 February – Latin februa – Roman festival of purification held this month.

3 March – Mars – Roman god of war.

4 April – Latin Aprilis (to open).

5 May – Various theories. Perhaps from Maia, Roman goddess of spring and growth.

6 June – May come from Juno, chief Roman goddess. Or perhaps from juniores (Latin for young men) to whom month was dedicated.

c Re-write the sentences, using other words and phrases for the parts underlined, but keeping the same meaning.

1 Our names for the months are based on the Roman.

2 The earliest Roman calendar known to us consisted of ten months.

3 January and February were added later.

4 The old Roman calendar was not very accurate.

5 The Romans added extra days every other year.

6 The Julian calendar was a big improvement on the old one.

d Adjectives

The words Julian and Gregorian are adjectives derived from people's names. Write the adjectives formed from these names:

Arthur, Edward, Elizabeth, James, George, Victoria, Napoleon, Moses, Francis, Cyril.

(The Russian alphabet is attributed to St Cyril and derives its name from his.)

e

1 Write out the old rhyme that tells how many days there are in each month.

2 Which of these were, or will be, leap years:
   1600   1700   1800   1900   2000   2100?

3 In order to shorten the year by 11 days what would be the date, in Britain, on the day after 2 September 1752?

4 Three of these periods of time are based on natural units:
   Day   Week   Month   Year.

   Explain what each natural unit is and say which period is the odd one out.

Using words

Using words effectively involves choosing just the right word to convey a particular meaning. Each of the following illustrations shows a different way of looking at something, and it is possible to use a different word each time to say what kind of looking it is.

a Write the sentences, completing each with a word that means looked or looked at. Use a different word each time.

1 The doctor _____ the patient.
2 Nigel _____ through the keyhole.
3 A number of men _____ the proposed building site.
4 Karen _____ briefly at her watch.
5 We _____ the programme with great interest.
6 The rescue team _____ for survivors.
7 Colonel Fanshaw _____ the regiment.
8 The man at the turnstile _____ our tickets.
9 I _____ in amazement at what I saw.

b Re-write the sentences, using other words and phrases in place of those underlined but keeping the same meaning.

1 The rich people looked down on their poorer neighbours.
2 Mrs White looked after our cat when we went on holiday.
3 The detectives looked into the robbery.
4 The recruits were told to look sharp.
5 All the parishioners looked up to the vicar.
6 'Look out!' he shouted. 'There's a car coming.'
7 The grocer said that trade was looking up.
8 We didn't like the look of the food.
9 Julie doesn't look herself this morning.
10 'I shall look for an improvement in our next game,' said the trainer.

c Adjectives

Write adjectives (a different one for each) that could be used to describe these things.

1 a snowfall
2 a cloud
3 a drink
4 a coat
5 a story
6 a cake
7 a problem
8 a breeze
9 a chair
10 a valley
11 a knife
12 a voice
13 a neighbour
14 a kitten
15 a road
16 a hill
17 a dress
18 a journey

d Re-write the sentences, using simpler words or phrases in place of the words underlined but keeping the same meaning.

1 After some time the conflagration was extinguished.
2 They were exhausted by the time they reached the summit.
3 We discovered a narrow passage concealed behind the panel.
4 She opened the volume at the appropriate page.
5 We purchased sufficient food to last for a week.
6 He attempted to surmount all obstacles.
7 We encountered inclement weather when we reached the hills.
8 The two cars departed simultaneously.
9 The lecturer demonstrated how the chemical was manufactured.
10 The patient adopted a sedentary posture.

e

What other shorter, simpler words could be used in place of these?

circular   inaccurate   intoxicated
antiquated   benevolent   corpulent   affluent
impecunious   tranquil   avaricious

Place names travel

Just as European languages have been taken to many parts of the world so also have European place names. Very often these names tell us something about early settlers and where they came from. Perhaps the settlers liked to use some familiar names to remind them of the homes they had left behind.

Most of the place names that have travelled are British, French, Spanish, Portuguese and Dutch and many examples of these can be found in the New World.

A number of New World place names have distant associations with royalty. New York (formerly New Amsterdam) was named for the Duke of York, later James II. Louisiana was named after King Louis XIV of France. North and South Carolina take their names from the Latin form of Charles, being named after Charles I. A daughter of Queen Victoria gave her first name (Louise) to a lake in Canada and her third (Alberta) to a Canadian province.

There are many Spanish names in both North and South America. The words Los Angeles are part of a long name, meaning Our Lady the Queen of the Angels of Porciuncula. No doubt you can work out the meaning of Puerto de San Francisco, El Paso del Norte and what we call these places now. Las Vegas simply means the meadows.

But not all names in America are borrowed from Europe. Many are of Indian origin. These include Saskatchewan, Ontario, Winnipeg, Toronto, Connecticut, Missouri, Wichita and Chicago.

a Write a sentence for each answer.

1 From which European countries are many American place names taken?
2 What was the previous name of New York?
3 After whom was New York named?
4 How did Louisiana get its name?
5 Which states of the U.S.A. are named after Charles I?
6 How does Lake Louise get its name?
7 How does the province of Alberta get its name?
8 What do the words Los Angeles mean?
9 What do the words Las Vegas mean?
10 What is the origin of the names Ontario, Toronto, Missouri and Wichita?

b Using the information given, write sentences telling how the following states in the U.S.A. got their names. Avoid beginning each sentence in the same way.

1	Maryland	Queen Henrietta Maria, wife of Charles I.
2	Vermont	French vert (green) and mont (mountain).
3	Washington	George Washington, first president of U.S.
4	Maine	Probably from mainland. To distinguish mainland from offshore islands.
5	Iowa	Indian word – obscure meaning.
6	Alaska	Aleutian word meaning mainland. (The Aleutians live on islands off coast of Alaska.)
7	Oregon	Perhaps from ouragan (French for hurricane).
8	Illinois	French form of Indian tribal name.
9	Utah	Ute (Indian tribe).
10	Montana	Spanish word meaning mountainous.

c Write the sentences, putting the right parts together.

1	Hudson Bay	is French for Mount Royal.
2	The name Montreal	is named after Elizabeth I of England.
3	The port of San Diego	takes its name from an Indian word.
4	The city of Ottawa	is named after a Spanish saint.
5	The state of Virginia	is called after an English explorer.

d A puzzle

Find the names of the U.S. states hidden in these sentences. Part of sentence no. 1 is underlined to help you.

1 The poor result exasperated the team manager.
2 A machine was installed for washing tons of coal.
3 Mary landed at Southampton.
4 The flight to Rio was delayed because of fog.
5 We shall cover the floor with mats until lino is available.
6 There is an enigma in each sentence.

e

1 Suggest how these American place names came about. New Hampshire, San Jose, Chattanooga, Baton Rouge, Pittsburgh.
2 Name any other parts of the world where there are towns or cities that have these British names: Ayr, Boston, Cambridge, Halifax, Hamilton, Hastings, Ipswich, Kingston, Launceston, London, Nelson, Newcastle, Perth, Richmond, Roxburgh, Stratford, Tamworth, Warwick, Wellington, Windsor.

Names of countries

The Roman world

The countries of the world have acquired their names in various ways. Many have historical associations of some sort, often being based on old names or connected with events of long ago.

A number of names go back to Roman times. For example, the word Italy comes from the Roman name Italia, though this was then applied only to the southern part of the Italian peninsula. Romania, the most obvious legacy of Roman occupation, simply means land of the Romans. The Roman province of Hispania gives us our word Spain and the Spanish España. Portugal was known to the Romans as Lusitania, but their name for the town of Oporto was Portus Cale and it is this that is the origin of the name Portugal.

Some countries take their names from people. Colombia, in South America, is one of many places in the New World called after Christopher Columbus. The name America is derived from Amerigo Vespucci, an explorer who claimed he had discovered the New World. The name was first given only to South America but gradually came to be used for the north as well.

The names of some countries have been made out of other names joined together. When the Czechs and the Slovaks joined to form a new independent country they called it Czechoslovakia. The union of Tanganyika and Zanzibar gave us Tanzania. Pakistan is an acronym combining parts of the names Punjab, Afghan frontier, Kashmir, Sind and Baluchistan.

a Write a sentence for each answer.

1 What is the origin of the name Italy?

2 What does the word Romania mean?

3 Explain how we get the word Spain.

4 What did the Romans call Portugal?

5 How did Portugal get its present name?

6 After whom is Colombia named?

7 How did America get its name?

8 Explain how Czechoslovakia got its name.

9 What country was formed from the union of Tanganyika and Zanzibar?

10 Explain how the name Pakistan was formed.

b Re-write each of these sentences in a different way, beginning with the words given. Some re-wording and re-arranging will be necessary.

1 The countries of the world have acquired their names in various ways.

There are various ways _____.

2 The word Italy comes from the Roman name Italia.

The Roman name Italia _____.

3 The Roman province of Hispania gives us our word Spain.

Our word Spain _____.

4 The American continent derives its name from Amerigo Vespucci.

Amerigo Vespucci _____.

5 Amerigo Vespucci claimed he had discovered the New World.

The discovery of the New World _____.

c Using the information given, write sentences telling how these countries got their names. Avoid beginning each sentence in the same way.

1 Ecuador — Spanish for equator. Equator passes through Ecuador.

2 Bolivia — After Simon Bolivar – Venezuelan general – helped Spanish colonies in S. America gain independence.

3 Chile — Indian word chilli meaning 'place where the land ends'.

4 Canada — Indian word Kanata or Kanada meaning a village or group of huts.

5 France — Franks – group of tribes who attacked Roman province of Gaul in 486 – set up kingdom there.

d At different times some countries have been known by different names. Write the alternative names for these countries.

1 Eire
2 Abyssinia
3 Netherlands
4 U.S.S.R.
5 Persia
6 United Arab Republic
7 Bechuanaland
8 Siam
9 Ceylon
10 Formosa

e Write the names of these countries in English:

1 Suisse, Schweiz or Svizzera
2 Belgique or Belgie
3 Deutschland
4 Osterreich
5 España
6 Danmark
7 Island
8 Sverige
9 Norge
10 Nederland

Practice pages

a Write the sentences, putting in apostrophes to show possession.

1 The ladys coats were in her wardrobe.
2 The ladies coats were in their cloakroom.
3 The childrens playground has been resurfaced.
4 The doors of the mens changing room were locked.
5 The womans car was parked outside her house.
6 The womens clothes are on the first floor.
7 The play was performed in the Infants hall.
8 There were boxes of apples and oranges outside the greengrocers shop.
9 We heard the sound of horses hoofs in the distance.
10 Simons dog has hurt its paw.

b Write sentences telling how we get the names of these months, using the information given. Avoid beginning each sentence in the same way.

1 July   After Julius Caesar. Previously Quintilis (meaning fifth) – fifth month of old Roman calendar.
2 August   After Emperor Augustus. Formerly Sextilis (sixth) – sixth month of old Roman calendar.
3 September Latin septem (seven) – seventh month of old Roman calendar.
4 October   Latin octo (eight).
5 November   Latin novem (nine).
6 December   Latin decem (ten).

c Write the sentences, choosing the best words from those in brackets. The more familiar words will help you decide what the harder words mean.

1 At the conclusion of the meeting everyone left the hall.
Conclusion means (beginning, middle, end).
2 The mob dispersed when the mounted police arrived.
Dispersed means (scattered, gathered, disappeared).
3 The game of golf originated in Scotland in about 1100.
Originated means (organised, began, reached).
4 The customers complained about the exorbitant prices.
Exorbitant means (low, high, exact).
5 One member expressed dissent, but everyone else was in favour.
Dissent means (decision, disagreement, agreement).

d Plurals

Write the plurals of these words:

1 story   5 motto   9 handkerchief
2 storey   6 solo   10 branch
3 radius   7 shelf   11 tax
4 cactus   8 dwarf   12 sheep

e   Using the information given, write sentences telling how the following states in the U.S.A. got their names. Avoid beginning each sentence in the same way.

1   Texas   Spanish pronunciation of Tejas – Indian word meaning friends or allies.

2   Missouri   From Missouri river. Missouri – probably from Indian word meaning 'town of the big canoes'.

3   Delaware   From Delaware Bay – after Lord De La Warr, governor of Virginia.

4   Georgia   After George II of England from whom settlers received their charter, 1732.

5   Pennsylvania   Means Penn's wood. (Sylvanus is Latin for wood.) William Penn founded colony 1681.

f   A puzzle

Find the names of the U.S. states hidden in these sentences:

1   The Gala skating rink was opened by the Mayor.
2   We shall miss our island holiday this year.
3   The plane flew over Mont Blanc.
4   At night there were more gondolas on the canal.
5   Louis, Ian and Albert were cousins.

g   Re-write the sentences, using other words and phrases for the parts underlined but keeping the same meaning.

1   Many loan words are now extensively used in everyday speech.
2   A number of New World place names have associations with royalty.
3   New York was formerly known as New Amsterdam.
4   Many place names in America are of Indian origin.
5   The countries of the world have acquired their names in various ways.

h   Give brief details of the things that take their names from these places:

1   Canary Islands   6   Champagne
2   Jaffa   7   Gorgonzola
3   Rugby   8   Stilton
4   Badminton   9   Oporto
5   Madeira   10   Panama

i   How much can you remember?

Write a sentence for each answer.

1   Who was Tyr?
2   Who was Saturn?
3   After which heavenly bodies did the Romans name the days?
4   In what ways was the early Roman calendar not very accurate?
5   What was unusual about the Roman god Janus?
6   Who was Mars?
7   What is the origin of the name Vermont?
8   Where does the word Spain come from?
9   Which explorer gave his name to the New World?
10   After whom is the country of Bolivia named?

j   Add -ing to each of these words, making any other changes in the spelling that are necessary.

(**Notice** bring **becomes** bringing
        shine **becomes** shining
        rub   **becomes** rubbing)

1	mean	8	write	15	choose
2	use	9	keep	16	arrange
3	run	10	replace	17	wait
4	make	11	begin	18	hit
5	put	12	explain	19	hunt
6	shop	13	indicate	20	hop
7	have	14	try	21	hope

Signs and notices

Signs and notices play an important part in helping us to find our way along roads, round towns and in buildings. They are used in shops and places of entertainment to persuade us to buy things or to draw our attention to a film or public performance. Signs and notices should be clear, not too long, informative and placed where people can easily read them. Ideally, they shouldn't be too numerous or people will be bewildered rather than helped.

Most signs and notices convey their meanings satisfactorily, but it is always interesting to discover any that are unusual in some way or other. For example, a notice on the window of an empty shop saying

> THE OUTSIZE DEPARTMENT HAS MOVED
> TO LARGER PREMISES

may amuse as well as inform customers.

Some signs are unintentionally ambiguous. Thus, a notice in a hotel saying

> SMOKING CAN BE DANGEROUS –
> PLEASE USE ASHTRAYS

can be interpreted in more than one way. The same applies to

> ALL MEAT IN THIS SHOP IS FROM LOCAL FARMERS
> KILLED ON THE PREMISES

– a notice in a butcher's shop window.

In other instances a joke or double meaning is deliberate, as in this notice displayed in a driving school office:

> IF YOUR WIFE WANTS TO LEARN TO DRIVE,
> DON'T STAND IN HER WAY.

And we may be sure of the intention behind the notice on the bowl of water put out by the thoughtful owner of a pet shop. This simply said:

> HOT DOGS ONLY.

a Write a sentence for each answer.

1 In what way do signs and notices help us?

2 In what sort of places are signs and notices used?

3 What qualities and features should signs and notices have?

4 Why shouldn't there be too many signs and notices?

5 What does an outsize department sell?

6 Explain the connection between 'outsize' and 'larger'.

7 Write an improved version of the notice about smoking.

8 Explain the double meaning in the butcher's notice.

9 Explain the double meaning in the driving school notice.

10 Do you think that many dogs would see the point of the notice on the bowl of water?

b Write the words from the passage opposite that mean the same as

1 giving information   5 explained
2 confused   6 intentional
3 carry   7 shown
4 having two meanings   8 purpose.

c Here are some signs and notices where there is a deliberate play on words, such as a double meaning or pun. In each case explain what the play on words is.

1 Notice on door of explosives store:
PLEASE KNOCK GENTLY.

2 Sign outside museum:
REMAINS TO BE SEEN.

3 On a church notice board:
WE ARE AT YOUR SERVICE. WILL YOU BE AT OURS?

4 Notice in dress shop window:
COME INSIDE AND MEET OUR PRINTS CHARMING.

5 On window of cut-price shop:
USE OUR PAPERWEIGHTS TO KEEP YOUR BILLS DOWN.

d Here are some signs and notices where there is an unintentional ambiguity or play on words. Explain what this is in each case.

1 Notice on newsagent's door:
PAPER BOYS AND GIRLS WANTED.

2 Notice near construction site:
HEAVY PLANT CROSSING ROAD.

3 On school notice board:
SCHOOL WILL BE CLOSED NEXT WEEK FOR A FORTNIGHT.

4 In restaurant window:
OPEN SEVEN DAYS.

5 In chemist's shop:
WE DISPENSE WITH ACCURACY.

e

1 Comment on these signs and notices, saying what they mean and what they are supposed to mean. Write an improved version in each case.

a In a shopkeeper's window:
SAUSAGE ROLL'S FOR SALE

b At the side of the road running alongside the beach at a holiday resort.
PLEASE DRIVE SLOWLY CHILDREN

2 What do you think is the purpose of this notice, painted on the back of a bus in not very large letters?
IF YOU CAN READ THIS, YOU'RE TOO CLOSE

Word puzzles

a Crossword puzzles are one of the most popular of
   word puzzles. The first one appeared in a New
   York newspaper in 1913, but it wasn't until 1924
   that one was published in a British newspaper.
   Many of the clues in crossword puzzles are in the
   form of anagrams or puns.
   Make a copy of the following grid and fill in the
   words from the clues below.

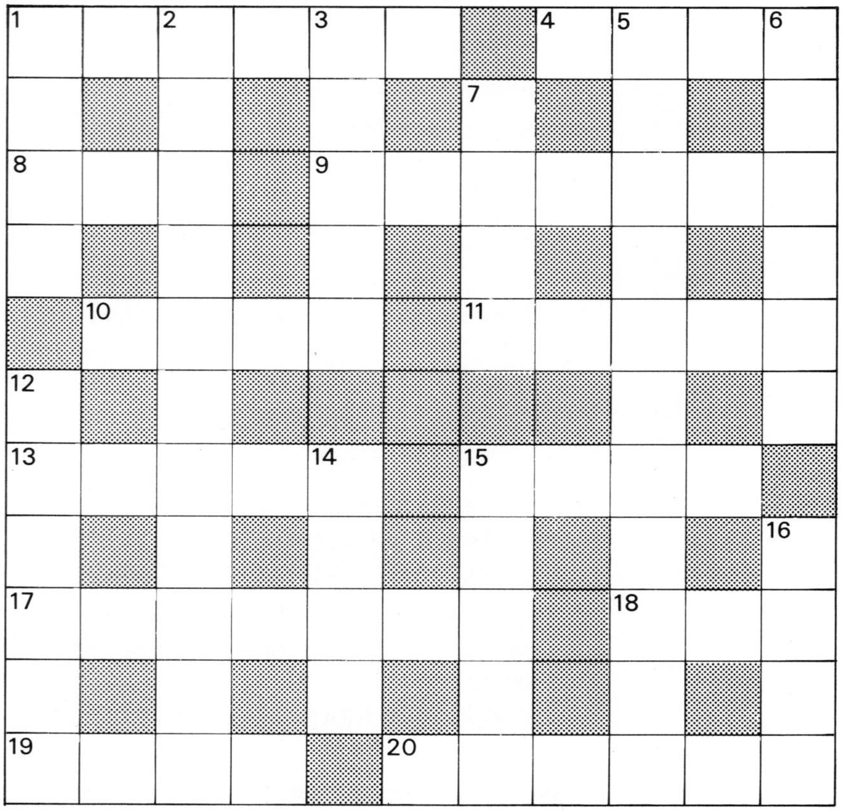

ACROSS

1 Secret writing or the symbol O. (To decipher
   this clue take two letters from one of these
   words.)
4 The noise made by a snake.
8 A writing instrument or an enclosure for
   animals.
9 A building where plays are performed.
10 A heavenly body giving out its own light.
11 A short poem or song. (Used in the plural to
   mean the words of a popular song.)
13 A sudden loud noise. A violent collision.
15 There are eight of them in this clue.
17 The first letter of a person's name.
18 Something to play with.
19 A series of notes making a melody or air.
20 A building used for public worship.

DOWN

1 To imitate or make a likeness of something.
2 The use of full stops, commas etc. in a piece
   of writing.
3 To go into.
5 A person who translates speech from one
   language to another.
6 Words that are spoken. (The word required
   appears in the clue above.)
7 A sudden, sharp, loud cry.
12 A shortened form of manuscript.
14 To shout to someone or a word meaning
   frozen rain.
15 A language spoken in Wales.
16 A story or legend.

b Palindromes

A palindrome is a word, sentence or verse that reads the same backwards as well as forwards. Write the answers to match these definitions. Each word should be a palindrome.

1 A cloth put under the chin to keep the clothes clean.
2 The past tense of 'do'.
3 Something done: often an act of courage or skill.
4 A female sheep.
5 An Eskimo canoe with an enclosed deck.
6 A familiar way of saying father.
7 The plural of solo.
8 Something placed in the mouth to keep a person silent.
9 The sound of a horn or whistle, – usually much less than a full blast.
10 A large horizontal propeller that spins round above the body of a helicopter.

c Complete these palindromes. The number of lines indicates the number of words to be added.

1 Was it a cat _____ _____?
2 Rise to vote, _____.
3 A man, a plan, a canal: _____.
4 Step on _____ _____.
5 Never odd _____ _____.
6 Madam, I'm _____.
7 Draw pupil's _____ _____.
8 Live on, Time, _____ _____ _____.
9 Able was I ere _____ _____ _____.
10 Now stop, Major-General, _____ _____ _____ _____ _____?

d Anagrams

An anagram is a word or phrase whose letters can be re-arranged to make another word or words. Re-arrange the letters of the words on the left to match the definitions in brackets.

1 west   (a dish of meat and vegetables cooked slowly)
2 balm   (a young sheep)
3 leap   (an urgent request, oftern for mercy or leniency)
4 save   (a receptacle for holding flowers)
5 tower   (the past tense of write)
6 stake   (a slice of meat – usually beef)
7 sheet   (plural of 'this')
8 hinge   (the sound made by a horse)
9 occurs (a small spring flower)
10 pierce (directions for preparing food)

e Here is a Latin palindrome:

SATOR AREPO TENET OPERA ROTAS

(It means 'The sower, Arepo, holds the wheels at work.') It is unusual because it can be made into a palindromic word square. To do this, draw a copy of the grid below and arrange the letters, one in each square, beginning at the top left-hand corner. What do you notice about the ways in which the words can be read?

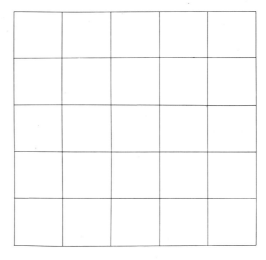

Words that may be confused

The English language contains a large number of words that may be easily confused with each other. Some (such as stationary and stationery, practice and practise, whole and hole) sound exactly alike. In other cases (such as sceptre and spectre, bugler and burglar, libel and liable) there is only a slight difference in sound. Mistakes made between such pairs of words can sometimes produce quite absurd effects.

a Write the sentences, choosing the correct word from each pair in brackets.

1 The doctor put the (thermometer, barometer) in my mouth.
2 The (pylon, python) is one of the world's largest snakes.
3 A (sturgeon, surgeon) is a doctor who performs operations.
4 A party of sailors boarded the Spanish (galleon, gallon).
5 There were two (taxis, taxes) waiting outside the station.
6 Another name for caterpillar is (larva, lava).

7–12 Now write six more sentences, using each of the words from the above pairs that you did not use in sentences 1–6.

b Re-write the sentences correctly, replacing each wrong word with a word that is not unlike it in general shape or sound.

1 The neglected wound had turned sceptic.
2 I waited outside the telephone chaos.
3 The patient was suffering from a rare melody.
4 Mrs Moore bought a cartoon of ice-cream.
5 A glacier is a person who puts glass in windows.

c Re-write the sentences, choosing the correct word from those in brackets.

1 I decided to (accept, except) the invitation.
2 The boy's handwriting was (eligible, illegible).
3 A (sheik, shriek) is an Arab chief.
4 We saw a short (excerpt, expert) from the play.
5 The cabbage was strained through a (calendar, colander).

d Here is a rather different problem. This time the mistakes are not confined to one word in each case but are the result of the choice and arrangement of words. Write an improved version of each sentence.

1 'May I try that dress on in the window?' she asked.
2 Mrs Ward stuffed the turkey with her husband.
3 Mr and Mrs Scott had lived in the street for ten years.
4 Yesterday we had Auntie Jane for dinner.
5 Mr Jackson teaches the piano.
6 There was no one to cook for us so we had to cook ourselves.
7 Mr Brown is a teacher and his wife.
8 Father cooked the breakfast while we sat round the table and ate it.
9 The batsman wore a cap to keep off the sun.
10 'I'm not very hungry,' said Simon. 'I don't feel like a dinner.'
11 He was unable to play with his injured knee.
12 The soldiers wore Balaclava helmets to keep themselves warm at the front.

e Write pairs of sentences to show the difference in meaning between these pairs of words.

irrelevant	and	irreverent
interpret	and	interrupt
prosecuted	and	persecuted
alligator	and	allegory
epitaph	and	epithet

Names

Nowadays we are accustomed to the fact that most people have at least two names, a first name or Christian name which is personal to them, and a surname or family name which they take from their parents and share with any brothers and sisters.

Up to about the time of the Middle Ages, however, each person had just one name. In the first place these were made from ordinary words and were often descriptive in meaning.

When the Normans came to England they brought their names with them and some of these became more popular than the Old English names. William, Robert, Charles, Richard and Geoffrey were all introduced by the Normans. Later, many Bible names became popular. Names such as Mary, Elizabeth, Hannah, John and David all came from this source. Greek and Latin names include Margaret, Patricia, Barbara, Helen, Alexander and George. Often we find masculine and feminine forms of the same name, as with Paul and Pauline, Julian and Julie, Stephen and Stephanie. Sometimes an old name is shortened or altered in some way. Belinda then becomes Linda, while from Christina we get Tina.

Second names came into use during the Middle Ages. These were useful to distinguish between people of the same name. The next step was for the second name to be passed on from one generation to the next, so becoming a family name.

a Write a sentence for each answer.

1 What are first names sometimes called?
2 What is another name for surname?
3 How were names formed in the first place?
4 Mention some names that were introduced by the Normans.
5 Mention some Biblical names that we use.
6 Make a list of names that come from Greek and Latin.
7 Write the feminine forms of Paul, Julian and Stephen.
8 Explain how we get the names Linda and Tina.
9 When did second names come into use?
10 In what way were second names useful?

b Common nouns and proper nouns

All nouns are names but we can group many of them as either common nouns or proper nouns. A common noun refers to a class of things and not to an individual object or person. A proper noun is the name of a particular thing or person and should be written with a capital letter.

Write these headings in your note book or exercise book:

Common nouns   Proper nouns

Then write these words under the right heading. Proper nouns should have capital letters.

sarah, uncle, president, everest, wednesday, macbeth, composer, queensland, title, nigeria, jeremy, february, saint, auckland, university, mountain, mississippi, prayer, river, planet.

c Names from people

The names of some things are derived from the names of the people who discovered them or are associated with them. Write the words we get from these names and say what each thing is:

1 André Ampère   6 Samuel Colt
2 Francis Beaufort   7 Earl of Derby
3 Louis Braille   8 Rudolf Diesel
4 Robert Bunsen   9 Joseph Guillotin
5 Earl of Cardigan   10 John McAdam

d A puzzle

Here are the names of some fictitious characters and the work they do. Write them out, re-arranging the occupations and activities in the correct order. Then write brief explanations as to how these people got their names.

1 Walter Wall   – the authority on sea birds
2 Albert Ross   – the bedding saleswoman
3 Horace Cope   – the continental waiter
4 Ida Downes   – the carpet salesman
5 Roland Butter – the astrologer

e Surnames came about in a variety of ways, many coming from the following:

place names

names or descriptions of a locality or district

names of occupations

names of parents

nicknames.

Suggest how these names may have come into being.

Baker   Forest   York   Armstrong   Johnson

Joseph Guillotin

The language of headlines

World sugar exporters stick to their guns

BLACK MAGIC LIFTS ALBION

MAFIA MOBSTERS MUSCLE IN ON THE SAINT

Madame la Guillotine splits public opinion

Still no cure for Anfield disease

Giving an eye to vandals

Export of arms banned

The pros and cons of going to pot

There are headlines in books and there are spoken headlines on radio or television that give a summary of the news, but here we are concerned with headlines that appear in newspapers or on placards. What we are looking at is whether some headlines may be a little too sensational, relying too much on certain well-used words and phrases.

Part of the trouble stems from the nature of headlines. They have to be brief, easily-read and, if possible, interesting so that we are enticed to read on. Headlines on placards are a form of advertising and are no doubt used to whet our appetites in the hope that we buy a copy of the newspaper.

A careful look at a few headlines soon reveals the style and pattern that many of them follow. To save space and arouse interest short, forcible words and abbreviations are often used. A demonstration is always a 'demo', an earthquake becomes a 'quake', while helicopter may be shortened to 'copter' and operation to 'op'. Any proceedings become a 'move', and a prohibition is a 'ban'. Any urgent journey is nearly always a 'dash', and if it is done to rescue someone it becomes a 'mercy dash'. Any manager is a 'boss' or 'chief' – perhaps even a 'top boss'. Industrial agreement is usually 'peace', weapons are 'arms', business transactions become 'deals', investigations are 'probes' and any unauthorised disclosure of information is a 'leak'.

a Write a sentence for each answer. (except no. 6)

1 Mention the different kinds of headlines that we come across.

2 Write out the part that means that headlines need to be short.

3 Why are headlines made to sound interesting?

4 What purpose is served by headlines on placards?

5 Why are short, forcible words and abbreviations used in headlines?

6 Write in full: demo, quake, copter, op.

7 Which headline word means 'something that is prohibited'?

8 What kind of event is a 'mercy dash'?

9 Which words are used in place of manager?

10 What headline words are used for (a) a business transaction, and (b) an inquiry?

b Write suitable headlines, along the lines already mentioned, for these news items. A suggested length for each headline is given in brackets.

1 There are new proceedings under way to prohibit the holding of a public demonstration. (five words)

2 A helicopter has made an emergency rescue flight. (four words)

3 The head of British Rail is involved in discussions to restore industrial harmony. (five words)

4 An inquiry is being held into an armaments transaction. (three words)

5 An unauthorised disclosure of information has had a bad effect on share prices. (three or four words)

c Using ordinary plain English, explain the meaning of each of these headlines so as to show what happened.

1 Police quiz soccer fans.

2 Man held in drugs haul.

3 Talks dashed by new row.

4 Union raps jobs probe.

5 Chief quits after shock report.

d Here are some headlines that have an ambiguity or double meaning. In each case say what the intended meaning is and then explain the other interpretation that is possible.

1 MP supports new bridge.

2 Minister acts to save theatre.

3 Police in race move.

4 Man stole government report.

5 Japanese in car talks.

e Not all newspaper headlines follow the same well-worn paths. Here are two examples that show a little more enterprise in their use of language. Explain how the choice and use of words makes them more interesting

a Headline for a report on a mass inoculation at a public school:
   Jabs for the boys

b Headline for a report on a football match in which a well-known goalkeeper unexpectedly conceded three goals:
   Shilton's net losses

Practice pages

a   Re-write the sentences, choosing the correct word from those in brackets.

1   When the volcano erupted, hot (lava, larva) poured out of the crater.
2   The archaeologists (evacuated, excavated) a neolithic site.
3   A (century, sentry) is a period of one hundred years.
4   The singer had a large (reservoir, repertoire) of songs.
5   The choir sang a (discount, descant) to the second verse.

b   Notices

Punctuate these notices so as to improve the sense.

1   SLOW OLD PEOPLE CROSSING ROAD
2   NOKOFF RELIEVES COUGHS FROM YOUR CHEMIST
3   ANTIQUES PLEASE DRIVE IN
4   GUARD DOGS KEEP AWAY
5   POLICE NOTICE NO PARKING
6–10   Write five sentences to explain what the notices mean as they are above.

c   Palindromes

Write the answers to match the definitions. Each word should be a palindrome.

1   Flat, even or horizontal.
2   Twelve o'clock midday.
3   A quick look, perhaps through a narrow opening.
4   A raised deck at the stern of a ship.
5   The use of radio waves to find position, direction and range.

d   Anagrams

Re-arrange the letters of the words on the left to match the definitions in brackets.

1   cafe   (the front part of the head)
2   hire   (someone who inherits something)
3   late   (a story, yarn or narrative)
4   keen   (the joint between the shin bone and the thigh)
5   cried   (a drink made from apple juice)
6   ample   (a kind of tree)
7   canoe   (a large expanse of salt water)
8   models   (not often)
9   nicest   (a small animal with six legs)
10 roasting   (someone who plays the organ)

e   Common nouns and proper nouns

Write these headings in your note book or exercise book.

Common nouns   Proper nouns

Then write these words under the right heading. Proper nouns should have capital letters.

lake, panama, arabic, sea, explorer, tasmania, baltic, language, poet, michigan, sydney, sahara inventor, island, edison, desert, canal, city, tennyson, livingstone.

f   Names from people
Write the words we get from these names and say what each thing is:

1   Charles Macintosh   6   Adolphe Sax
2   Samuel Morse   7   Henry Shrapnel
3   George Pullman   8   Alessandro Volta
4   Samuel Plimsoll   9   James Watt
5   The Earl of   10   The Duke of
    Sandwich   Wellington

g A puzzle

Here are the names of some more fictitious characters and the work they do. Write them out, re-arranging the occupations and activities in the correct order. Then write brief explanations as to how these people got their names.

1 Ann Cuff   the successful horsewoman
2 Noah Drinkwater   the painter
3 Claire Round   the Scottish innkeeper
4 Matt Black   the ornithologist
5 Nesta Robins   the policewoman

h Headlines

Explain what each of these headlines is supposed to mean and then point out any other interpretations that are possible.

1 Police alert as river rises.
2 Doctors will leave warning.
3 Free education to cost $840 million a year.
4 Soccer fans charged.
5 Docks: Prime Minister steps in.

i How much can you remember?

Write a sentence for each answer.

1 What do we call a word, sentence or verse that reads the same backwards as well as forwards?
2 Which of these words are palindromes? – prop, minim, stunts, reader, deified, smart.
3 What do we call a word or phrase whose letters can be re-arranged to make another word or words. (For example, the letters of the word 'cautioned' can be re-arranged to make the word 'education'.)
4 In what form are many of the clues in crossword puzzles?
5 How were the names William, Robert, Charles, Richard and Geoffrey introduced into England?
6 Where did the names Mary, Elizabeth, Hannah, John and David come from?
7 What is a common noun?
8 What is a proper noun?
9 What is unusual or special about the names of these people: Louis Braille, Rudolf Diesel and John McAdam?
10 Name some of the ways in which surnames originated.

j Comment on these signs and notices, saying what they mean and what they are supposed to mean.

1 Notice outside tailor's shop:
       SALE. ALL SUITS SLASHED.
2 Notice in hotel bathroom:
       PLEASE DRAW BATH CURTAIN BEFORE USING IT.
3 Notice in zoo:
       PLEASE DO NOT FEED THE ANIMALS. ANY SUITABLE FOOD SHOULD BE GIVEN TO THE KEEPERS.
4 Notice on litter bin:
       PEOPLE WHO DO NOT PUT RUBBISH IN BINS PROVIDED WILL BE PROSECUTED.
5 Notice outside flower shop:
       FOR SALE: FRESH CUT.

k Write the sentences, choosing the best words from those in brackets.

1 Confusion between some pairs of words can produce absurd results.
Absurd means (bad, ridiculous, abnormal).
2 We are accustomed to people having at least two names.
Accustomed means (introduced, known, used).
3 Headlines may give brief summaries of the news.
Summaries means (outlines, accounts, stories).
4 An interesting headline may entice us to read further.
Entice means (force, provoke, tempt).
5 An interesting headline may whet our appetite for more.
Whet means (moisten, sharpen, prepare).

Letter writing

Letter writing is one of the oldest and most important means of communication. Read the two letters below and then answer the questions that follow.

123, Thornfield Crescent,
Oxford.
15th May 1978

Dear Mrs. Parker,
Thank you for sending the illustrated brochure. I would like to reserve two double bedrooms for the 19th – 26th August. I enclose a deposit. I wonder if you would be kind enough to tell me if pets are allowed at your hotel.

Yours sincerely.
Brian Matthews

**Clifftops Guest House
Minehead**

17th May 1978

Dear Mr. Matthews,

Thank you very much for your letter of 15th May and deposit, for which I enclose a receipt.

I have pleasure in reserving two double bedrooms for you for the week 19th–26th August.

Later on, perhaps you would be good enough to let me know what time you expect to arrive.

Yours sincerely,

Ann Parker.

a

1 Who has written to Mrs Parker?

2 Who has written to Mr Matthews?

3 Who lives at 123 Thornfield Crescent?

4 Where are the Matthews family going for their holidays?

5 When did Mr Matthews write to Mrs Parker asking her to reserve two rooms?

6 What did Mr Matthews send with his letter?

7 What did Mrs Parker send with her reply?

8 How can you tell that Mr Matthews and Mrs Parker had exchanged letters previously?

9 Mrs Parker forgot to mention something that she had been asked about. What was that?

10 What additional information has Mrs Parker asked to have?

b Read the following letter.

191 Townend Road
Wednesday

Dear Sir We want to know if you will come and mend the washing machine. There is a hole somewhere and on Monday it was all over the floor and even in the living room. It spoiled the carpet and we only had it last year. It cost ever such a lot of money. You should have seen the mess. Every time we use it the water comes out. My husband says it is a disgrace for a new thing to be like this so will you mend it for us and oblige.

Mrs Pool

1 Comment on the style and efficiency of the letter. Think of the person who will receive it. Does it tell him all he needs to know or anything he doesn't need to know?

2 Re-write the letter as you think it should have been. (Invent any facts and figures that you think would be needed.)

c Read this letter dealing with holiday plans made by two friends. (The address was correct, so only the main body of the letter is quoted.)

Dear James,

Thank you for your letter of the 16th May giving the time of our flight to Majorca. I note that the aircraft is due to take off at 1130 hours, so I suggest we arrive at the airport at 1030 sharp to allow time for handling of baggage, checking of travel documents, inspection of passports etc. I shall avail myself of the car parking facilities and then proceed to the main terminal where I hope to have the pleasure of meeting you.

Yours sincerely
Peter

1 Comment on the style and efficiency of this letter.

2 Re-write the letter in a more suitable style.

d Write a letter to your local electricity board suggesting that you have been overcharged for electricity. Give clear reasons why you think this is so. (Perhaps your cooking and heating are done by gas or maybe you are out of the house all day.) Compare the amount charged with the previous bill and ask if it will be possible for someone to investigate your complaint.

e Draw a rectangle about $5\frac{1}{2}$ inches by $3\frac{3}{4}$ inches (about 14 cm by $9\frac{1}{2}$ cm) in your note book or exercise book. Write a name and address on it as though it were an envelope to be posted. Leave about $1\frac{1}{2}$ inches (nearly 4 cm) clear right across the top.

(If you don't know anybody else's address, write your own name and address on the 'envelope'.)

REMEMBER to use the POST CODE

Mr John Saville
23 Jacobs Lane
ABINGDON
OXON.
OX16 4AR

Communication for the handicapped

People who are blind or deaf cannot use conventional means of communication. Fortunately, various ways have been devised to enable the blind to read and the deaf to understand what is said to them. These methods are quite difficult to learn and children who are blind or deaf are taught in special schools where they are given extra help with their problems.

Braille is a special kind of alphabet that enables the blind to read by touch. It is called after Louis Braille, who invented the system in about 1829. For a few years after that it was little used, but has since won universal acceptance. Braille utilizes various arrangements of raised dots on paper, the dots occupying some or all of the six positions in this pattern:

$$\begin{matrix} \bullet & \bullet \\ \bullet & \bullet \\ \bullet & \bullet \end{matrix}$$

Various arrangements of the dots represent different symbols. Of the 63 different arrangements of dots that are possible 26 are used for letters of the alphabet, the remaining 37 standing for numerals, punctuation, common words (such as the, of, and) and the commoner parts of words (such as ch, ed, ing).

A blind person reads by running the fingertips lightly over the dots. An experienced braille reader can read at a speed of about 200 words a minute.

A blind person can write by means of a braillewriter – a machine resembling a typewriter.

a Write a sentence for each answer.

1 What arrangements are made for the education of blind or deaf children?

2 What is braille?

3 Explain how braille gets its name.

4 What sort of dots are used to enable the reader to feel them?

5 What do the various arrangements of dots represent?

6 How many different arrangements of dots are possible?

7 What else do the dots stand for besides letters of the alphabet?

8 How does a blind person read?

9 How fast can an experienced braille reader read?

10 What sort of machine can a blind person use to write with?

b Write the words from the passage that mean the same as

1 customary or usual
2 world-wide
3 makes use of
4 stand for
5 characters, such as letters and figures
6 similar to.

c Words sometimes confused

Write the sentences, choosing the correct words from inside the brackets.

1 The children were (learned, taught) how to play the recorder.

2 An old proverb tells us that (practice, practise) makes perfect.

3 I asked David if I could (lend, borrow) his ruler.

4 'I think (its, it's) going to rain,' said Mother.

5 Because of the rain there were (less, fewer) people at the match.

d Write out the following as five sentences, putting in all necessary capital letters and punctuation marks.

people who are deaf can communicate by such means as lip reading sign language and the manual alphabet lip reading is difficult because there are instances when different words produce the same lip movements sign language consists of gestures some of which are in the form of a simple mime the manual alphabet is made by positioning the fingers and hands to stand for different letters so that words can be spelt out for those who are both deaf and blind the method of communication is by touch the speaker using his right hand to make signs on the left hand of the listener

e

1 Books printed in braille are bigger and more cumbersome than ordinary books. Suggest two reasons why this is so.

2 Many blind people learn to type, using a method known as 'touch typing'. What is 'touch typing' and why do you think it helpful for blind people to know how to do it?

3 Find out what you can about these two remarkable people:
   a Helen Keller
   b Joseph Hatton

Heraldry

Heraldry is a form of communication. When knights in full armour rode to battle they were not easy to recognise unless they had a distinctive design on their shields. The design was also carried on a knight's outer garment or surcoat, hence the term 'coat-of-arms', the word 'arms' meaning the designs and devices that were used.

The idea of using a personal design or emblem on shields probably began with the Crusades, when it would be useful for knights of different nationalities to carry some means of identification.

The first English king to have a coat of arms was Richard I in 1189. The lion of Scotland appeared as a heraldic symbol in 1222. By 1245 there were definite rules about the design and use of coats of arms, the king's officers in charge of such matters being called heralds.

A coat of arms and the surrounding parts is called an achievement of arms and consists of up to seven parts: shield, helmet, wreath, crest, mantling, motto and supporters. The helmet rests on top of the shield, except when the coat of arms belongs to a peer. (A peer has a coronet above the shield and the helmet is placed above the coronet.) The wreath fits round the top of the helmet and just below the crest. The mantling is an array of ornamental drapery around the shield. The motto, written on a scroll, is usually found below the shield. Supporters, if any, are usually placed one on each side of the shield.

a Write a sentence for each answer.

1 When did the idea of using coats of arms probably begin?

2 Who was the first English king to have a coat of arms?

3 When did the lion of Scotland appear as a heraldic symbol?

4 When did rules about coats of arms come into being?

5 What name is given to a coat of arms and surrounding parts?

6 Where does the helmet rest?

7 Where does the wreath fit?

8 What is the mantling?

9 Where is the motto usually found?

10 How do we get the word heraldry?

PREST D'ACCOMPLIR

b Fabulous beasts and creatures

Write sentences (one or more for each) based on the following outlines to describe various mythical beings used as heraldic designs. Avoid beginning each sentence in the same way and do not overwork the words fabulous and mythical. Use others, such as fabled, imaginary, legendary and fictitious as well.

1 dragon large, fierce, fire-breathing, reptile shape, massive claws, wings, long tail

2 pegasus a winged horse (Greek mythology), for a time ridden by Bellerophon

3 mermaid cross between person and fish; head and trunk of woman, tail of fish

4 phoenix unique bird, lives for 500–600 years, burns itself on funeral pyre, new phoenix rises from ashes etc.

5 unicorn body of horse, one straight horn projecting from forehead; tail like a lion's

c Puns

Many towns and cities have coats of arms, and sometimes the design is a pun on the town's name. For example, Cowbridge in South Glamorgan has a cow on a bridge on its coat of arms. Work out the names of the towns whose coats of arms bear the following devices

1 An ox fording a stream.

2 A maiden's head (on the crest).

3 A gateway on the shield and a goat's head on the crest.

4 A bee and an arrow.

5 Three swallows. (The French for swallow is hirondelle. The town is in Sussex.)

d Against each of these place names is a description of something that appears on its coat of arms. Explain why each device has a special meaning for the town that uses it.

1 Penzance a pirate and a fisherman as supporters

2 Stoke a potter of ancient Egypt

3 Newmarket a running horse

4 Banbury a lady mounted on a horse

5 Lambeth a mitre and archbishop's cross

QUOD:IMPROBUM TERRET:PROBO:PRODEST

e

1 Heraldry may have begun as part of the pageantry of the medieval tournament. Write a paragraph about the tournament, explaining what happened and who took part.

2 What two languages (apart from English) are most often used for mottoes?

3 What were the Crusades?

Signs and symbols

Signs and symbols are widely used to-day by all sorts of organisations such as companies, societies, industries, clubs, trades and crafts. Some are used by private firms, while others belong to government departments and nationalised industries.

The origin of many signs goes back to the days when few people could read. Traders and innkeepers would then draw attention to their goods and services by means of pictures. Often these were straightforward illustrations of what was for sale or else of something connected with it. Thus, a tobacconist's shop might be identified by a model or a picture of a pipe, while a tailor would display a picture of a pair of scissors.

As more people learned to read, the original purpose of many signs and symbols was lost and yet we come across them in all sorts of places – on the road, on buildings, on forms of transport, in books and on maps, on coins, pottery, silver ware and on school and club badges. People wear them on uniforms. Even cattle carry them sometimes. They appear on all sorts of manufactured articles in the form of trade-marks and are used on clothes to convey instructions about washing, bleaching, drying and ironing.

Many signs and symbols are in the form of a picture or emblem, but sometimes a word, letters or figures are added to give further information or to give a message that cannot easily be conveyed by a picture.

a Write a sentence for each answer.

1 What sorts of organisations use signs and symbols?

2 What is the origin of many of our signs and symbols?

3 When few people could read how would traders and innkeepers advertise their goods and services?

4 What sort of pictures were then used?

5 How might a tobacconist's shop be identified?

6 Who would display a picture of a pair of scissors?

7 What happened as more people learned to read?

8 Mention some places where signs and symbols are used?

9 What instructions do signs and symbols on clothes convey?

10 Why are words, letters and figures sometimes added to signs?

b Spelling

A letter has been missed out of each of these words. Write them correctly.

1 gover__ment   6 reco__nise
2 pe__ple   7 desi__n
3 s__issors   8 __reath (e.g. of flowers)
4 b__ildings   9 i__land
5 sc__ool   10 g__ard

c Write sentences (one or more for each) explaining where we are likely to see the following signs and symbols and what they mean.

1 Three stripes or chevrons on a sleeve.
2 Crossed swords above a date (such as 1066).
3 A red cross on a white background.
4 Five interlocking circles.
5 The letters AA, followed by one or more stars.

d Where do we see these signs and what do they mean? (█ = red.)

e Flags

A number of symbols or emblems appear on various national flags. On which flags do the following appear?

1 a red maple leaf on a white background
2 a dark blue wheel on a white central stripe
3 a red symbol of the sun on a white background
4 a gold hammer and sickle in the top left hand corner of a red flag
5 a red dragon on a white and green background

Communication without words

Many forms of communication involve words in some way, but sometimes it is easier and quicker to give information by means of signs and signals only. There are times when these can be more effective, being quicker to 'read' and, in some cases, visible over a greater distance than a message in words. A further advantage is that many signs and signals do not depend on knowledge of a particular language.

a Explain the meaning of each of the items shown above, numbering them 1 to 9. Explain what information is being given each time and under what circumstances. Say what advantage there is in each message being given in this particular way.

b Verbs from nouns

Write the sentences, filling each blank with a verb formed from the noun on the left.

communication 1 They _____ by means of sign language.

indication 2 The linesman waved his flag to _____ that the ball was out of play.

response 3 He didn't _____ to any of our signals.

gesture 4 The onlookers _____ by waving their arms.

reaction 5 She _____ by looking surprised.

c Write sentences to explain the meanings of these signs and gestures.

1 nodding the head in an up and down motion
2 the index or forefinger placed vertically across the closed lips
3 a clenched fist raised or shaken in someone's direction
4 a thumb (or both thumbs) pointing downwards
5 raising the eyebrows
6 shrugging the shoulders

d Describe suitable signs or gestures that might accompany these remarks.

1 Good-bye.   5 We've won!
2 I can't hear.   6 Turn it round.
3 Come over here.   7 I disagree.
4 Stop!   8 I feel rather tired.

e

1 What name do we give to a form of entertainment or game in which the actors or participants tell a story without using any words, but rely entirely on signs, gesture and movement?

2 Make a list of any other forms of non-verbal communication. Include any that use sound, but not actual speech, in one way or another. Think of any kinds of communication that are used (or have been used) in other countries (e.g. Switzerland) and in civilisations other than our own (e.g. North American Indian, African). Include any used by the armed services and any that are made by musical instruments.

Practice pages

a Making new words

Make new words by joining together a word from the first column with a word from the second column. For example, you could join type to writer to make typewriter.

1	type	spoken
2	inn	line
3	straight	quake
4	head	keeper
5	some	tips
6	out	wright
7	finger	writer
8	news	times
9	play	forward
10	earth	paper

b Letter writing

Here are some rather stilted phrases and expressions taken from some business letters. Re-write each in a less formal style.

1 Your letter of the 14th June to hand to which I now have the pleasure of replying.

2 As per your request we enclose herewith a copy of our catalogue.

3 We are in receipt of your esteemed order, for which many thanks.

4 This is to advise you that your account is overdue and we await the favour of a settlement.

5 We would beg you to inform us if the quality of our merchandise should fail to meet your expectations.

c Words sometimes confused

Write the sentences, choosing the correct words from inside the brackets.

1 We were (quiet, quite) satisfied with the arrangements.

2 Mother (bought, brought) a new hat to match her coat.

3 The sweets were divided (among, between) the four children.

4 The farmer found a tramp (laying, lying) on some straw in the barn.

5 They were anxious not to (lose, loose) their unbeaten record.

6 The painters are (hoping, hopping) to finish their work next week.

7 He had no (alibi, excuse) for being late for school.

d Spelling

A letter has been missed out of each of these words. Write them correctly.

1	ve__icle	6	antar__tic
2	c__aracter	7	__naw
3	m__ustache	8	r__ythm
4	r__ubarb	9	crum__
5	g__est	10	ec__o

e Heraldry

Against each of these place names is a description of something that appears on its coat of arms. Explain why each device has a special meaning for the place that uses it.

1 Wallsend — an eagle standing on a section of wall
2 Jarrow — an open book bearing the words BEDA HISTORIA ECCLESIASTICA
3 Egham — a picture of Magna Carta
4 Swindon — a railway locomotive
5 Worksop — one of the supporters is a forester holding a longbow

f Nouns, adjectives, verbs and adverbs

Say whether each underlined word in the sentences below is a noun, adjective, verb or adverb. Remember

A noun is the name of a person, place or thing.
An adjective describes a noun.
A verb expresses action (doing) or being.
An adverb tells us how, when or where something was done.

1 A piece of writing is a <u>permanent</u> record of something.
2 The <u>opening</u> of a letter is a kind of greeting.
3 Business letters should <u>keep</u> to the point.
4 Braille is a <u>special</u> kind of alphabet.
5 Braille consists of a number of raised <u>dots</u>.
6 A blind person runs the fingertips <u>lightly</u> over the dots.
7 Knights in full armour could not <u>easily</u> be recognised.
8 A knight's shield would help to <u>identify</u> him.
9 <u>Traders</u> used pictures to advertise their wares.
10 A <u>wide</u> range of feelings can be expressed by gestures and facial expressions.

g How much can you remember?

Write a sentence for each answer.

1 What do we call the special kind of alphabet that enables the blind to read by touch?
2 How do deaf people communicate?
3 Why is lip reading difficult?
4 What does sign language consist of?
5 What name is given to a knight's outer garment?
6 An achievement of arms consists of up to seven parts. What are their names?
7 In heraldry, what name is given to the figures usually placed one on each side of the shield?
8 What was the name of the winged horse in Greek mythology that was for a time the mount of Bellerophon?
9 What legendary creature has the head and trunk of a woman and the tail of a fish?
10 What advantages can there be in communicating by means of signs and signals instead of words?

h Write the proper nouns that are the names of the following. (All have been mentioned in this book so far.)

1 The great river that flows through Egypt.
2 The city where parchment was discovered.
3 The name of the language you are now reading.
4 The invaders who occupied much of Britain from A.D. 43 to about A.D. 410.
5 The people who invaded Britain in 1066.
6 The man who printed the 42-line Bible.
7 The most successful artificial language.
8 The day of the week called after Woden.
9 The wife of Odin in Norse mythology.
10 The seventh month of the old Roman calendar.
11 The name of the city formerly known as New Amsterdam.
12 The modern name for the Roman province of Lusitania.
13 The country that takes its name from the Spanish word for equator.
14 The country where the game of golf originated.
15 The state of the U.S.A. named after William Penn.

Using reference books

Some of the most useful reference books are encyclopaedias and dictionaries. An encyclopaedia is a book or books containing information on many subjects. Encyclopaedias can be read right through from cover to cover, but they are mainly intended for reference on particular points.

When using an encyclopaedia the first thing to know is how the information is arranged. The *Oxford Junior Encyclopaedia*, for example, is arranged in 12 main volumes and an index volume. Each of the main volumes covers a group of related subjects. Volume 1 (called Mankind) is about the people of the world, their customs, beliefs and religions. Volume 2 (called Natural History) is about the animals and plants in the world. Volume 3 (called The Universe) is about the countries of the world as well as stars, planets and other heavenly bodies. Within each volume the entries are arranged alphabetically.

In *Children's Britannica*, on the other hand, all the articles are arranged in alphabetical order throughout the 19 main volumes. (Volume 20 consists of an index and maps.) This arrangement puts Antelope in Volume 1 and Zebra in Volume 19, whereas in the *Oxford Junior Encyclopaedia* they are both in Volume 2 because they are both animals.

A dictionary is an alphabetically arranged list of words, usually with their meanings and other details. There are also subject dictionaries, such as dictionaries of people, places, music and battles.

a Write a sentence for each answer.

1 What is an encyclopaedia?

2 For what purpose are encyclopaedias mainly intended?

3 What is the first thing to know when using an encyclopaedia?

4 How many volumes has the *Oxford Junior Encyclopaedia*?

5 What does each of the main volumes cover?

6 What is *Oxford Junior Encyclopaedia* Volume 1 about?

7 What is *Oxford Junior Encyclopaedia* Volume 3 about?

8 How are the articles arranged in *Children's Britannica*?

9 What do *Children's Britannica* and *Oxford Junior Encyclopaedia* have in common?

10 What is a dictionary?

b When we look for information in an encyclopaedia we may not find anything under the first heading that we try. Sometimes it is necessary to look under a similar heading. For example, instead of looking for Football we may have to try Association Football, and instead of Caribou we may have to look for Reindeer.

Under what alternative headings could you look for information about these topics?

1	Milk	7	Vaccination
2	Alligators	8	Tasmania
3	Quilts	9	Engine driver
4	Mars	10	Flute
5	Orchards	11	Mastiff
6	Rooks	12	Terrapin

c The 12 main volumes of the Oxford Junior Encyclopaedia cover these subjects:

1	Mankind	7	Industry and
2	Natural History		Commerce
3	The Universe	8	Engineering
4	Communications	9	Recreations
5	Great lives	10	Law and Society
6	Farming and	11	Home and Health
	Fisheries	12	The Arts

In which volume would you look for these topics?

1	Spiders	7	Knitting
2	Marie Curie	8	Sculpture
3	Skating	9	Hong Kong
4	Television	10	Public Health
5	Norse myths	11	Catering
6	Dams	12	Potatoes

d The 20 volumes of Children's Britannica are arranged as follows:

1	Abbey–Arabs	11	London–Moss
2	Aran–Bee	12	Moth–Oyster
3	Beech–Build	13	Pacific–Pond
4	Bulbs–Chub	14	Pony–Rhyme
5	Church–Czech	15	Rice–Sedge
6	Dacca–Energy	16	Seed–Star
7	Engine–Furs	17	Starch–Toys
8	Gabon–Hedin	18	Tracks–Wall
9	Helen–Ivy	19	Walnut–Zurich
10	Jackal–Lomond	20	Index and Atlas

In which volumes of Children's Britannica would you look for the main entries about these topics?

1	The Battle of Hastings	7	Pompeii
2	Wild flowers	8	Budgerigars
3	Iron and Steel	9	Motor cars
4	Sewing	10	Joan of Arc
5	Sir Edward Elgar	11	Tournaments
6	Galaxies	12	Volcanoes

e

1 What are the advantages and disadvantages of (i) an encyclopaedia of several volumes, and (ii) a single-volume encyclopaedia?

2 Look at a multi-volume encyclopaedia for some information about who wrote it. Write down a summary of what you find.

Titles, contents and indexes

When we are choosing a book in a library or bookshop, we obviously cannot read right through it before deciding if it is suitable. We must use other ways to reach our decision.

Usually the title will be our first guide. It would be no good looking, for instance, in a book called *Four Bad Hens* if you wanted to know about diseases of poultry. Nor would you consult *Advanced Electrical Engineering* if you were only a beginner. Some books have attractive titles that don't give much away. *Top of the World* sounds as though it might be about Everest, but actually it's about an adventure at the top of a multi-storey office block.

A glance through the book is perhaps the next step. Is the reading matter too easy or too difficult? Are there any illustrations? Illustrations can help to bring an adventure story to life, but in books about birds or trees, for example, illustrations are indispensable. Scientific subjects often need diagrams and graphs, while geographical topics may require maps.

In the case of a non-fiction book it may be helpful to glance through the contents and index. The contents, at the front of a book, are usually a list of chapter headings, arranged in order of appearance. The index, placed at the back, is a list of people, places and things mentioned, arranged in alphabetical order.

a Write a sentence for each answer.

1 What will usually be our first guide when choosing a book?

2 Why do you think *Advanced Electrical Engineering* is unsuitable for beginners?

3 Why do you think *Top of the World* sounds as though it might be about Everest?

4 What purpose is served by illustrations in an adventure story?

5 In what sort of books are illustrations indispensable?

6 In what sort of books are diagrams often needed?

7 What sort of topics probably require maps?

8 What term is used to mean books that deal with facts?

9 Where are the contents of a book found and how are they arranged?

10 Where is the index in a book and how is it arranged?

b Read through this extract from a book and then answer the questions that follow.

Endeavour, Cook's ship, 56
Erebus, Franklin's ship, 75
Eriksson, Leif, Viking explorer, 16
Erik the Red, Viking explorer, 15
Eskimos, illus. 47, 85
Everest, Mount, exploration of, 88

1 From which part of the book is this taken? Give a reason for your answer.

2 Why are the words Endeavour and Erebus in italics?

3 Who was Leif Eriksson?

4 What kind of information is given about Eskimos?

5 Why does Mount Everest appear to have its name back to front?

c Write these headings in your note book or exercise book.

For younger readers   For older readers

Then write these titles (all fiction) under the correct heading.

The Little Dog, Knight Crusader, The Xanadu Manuscript, Two Bad Cats, Riders of the Storm, The Little Fire Engine, The Silver Christmas Tree, A Song for the Disco, Ever After, Five Dolls in a House, Mr Tall and Mr Small, A Journey of Many Sleeps

d Write these headings in your note book or exercise book.

Fiction   Non-fiction

Then write these titles under the correct heading.

The Arab World, Collecting from Nature, A Grass Rope, People of the World, Prince of the Jungle, All Made by Hand, Isle of the Sea Horse, The Dark is Rising, Escape into Daylight, Exploring the Seashore, Cannibal Adventure, Bridges and Tunnels

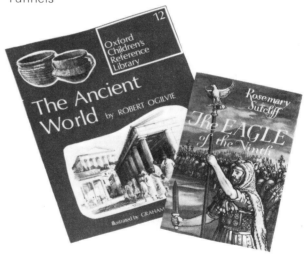

e Write these items as they would appear in an index:

Exploration of Australia   Hudson Bay
A Christmas Carol   David Livingstone
David Copperfield   The Wind in the
Vale of Evesham   Willows
Theory of Evolution   Sir Christopher Wren
Henry Hudson

Using books

Most people use books at some time or other. Sometimes we read or browse for pleasure. Sometimes we want to look up a particular item. Sometimes we study books for examination purposes.

At school young people are encouraged to find things out from books and perhaps write about what they have found. The least enterprising way of doing this is simply to copy from a book. A much better way is to read an account and then write it in your own words, perhaps summarising the main points. There are several ways of doing this.

One way is to read right through a passage once or twice so as to get an over-all picture of what it's about. Then close the book and write an account from memory, checking the result from the book after the writing is finished.

An alternative way is to read through a passage, making notes of the chief points as you go along. (Making notes is good practice in deciding which are the main things that you must include and which are the less important ones that can be left out.) Then put the book on one side and write your account from the notes you have prepared.

A third way is to read more than one account and then combine the best points of each in your own version. This method should give you a useful blend of facts and ideas that isn't a copy of anyone else's work.

a Write a sentence for each answer.

1 Mention some of the ways in which people use books.

2 In what way are young people at school encouraged to use books?

3 What is the least enterprising way of writing about something?

4 How is it helpful to read right through a passage first?

5 In what way is making notes good practice?

6 What use can be made of the notes that have been prepared?

7 What are the advantages of reading more than one account and then combining them in a piece of written work?

8 Which word means 'to read parts of a book here and there'?

9 Which word is used instead of 'account'?

10 Which word means 'mixture'?

b Summarise this passage, reducing it to about half its length.

The solar system consists of the sun and its 'family' of planets, moons, asteroids, comets and meteors. The sun is in the centre of our solar system. It is really a star. It is not by any means the brightest or the hottest star in the universe, but it is vitally important to us living here on earth because it gives us light and warmth. Without it the earth would be cold and dark. There would be no night and day and no spring, summer, autumn and winter. It would be cold and dark all the time in all countries. All the planets and other bodies that are in our solar system travel round the sun, although people used to think that the earth was at the centre of the solar system. The path that each of these bodies takes round the sun is called its orbit.

c Read through the passage on page 78 and then make notes of the part that describes the different ways of using information from books in our written work. (Lines 11 onwards.) Number your points 1, 2, 3 and begin each on a new line.

d Combine these two accounts into one so as to cover the main points.

Zebras are horse-like creatures standing about 1·2–1·5 m high at the shoulder. Now found only in Africa they are easily identified by their dark stripes on a lighter background, a feature that seems to serve as camouflage. Zebras eat grass and their chief enemy in the wild is the lion. Some species of zebra are now extinct.

Zebras are animals closely related to the horse. They were once found in Europe, Asia and North America but are now confined to Africa, south of the Sahara. There are several species, all with the familiar striped markings. Zebras are grazing animals living in small bands. Their chief enemy is the lion, but many have been killed by man.

e Write a list of rules and recommendations (up to about 10) telling people how to handle and look after books properly.

Using words

Each of the following illustrations shows some kind of movement, but it is possible to use a different word each time to say what the movement is.

a Write the sentences, completing each with a word that indicates movement. Use a different word each time.

1 The horses _____ across the downs.
2 The injured player _____ to the touchline.
3 Sally _____ into the water.
4 The car _____ to avoid a pedestrian.
5 The weary hikers _____ along the dusty road.
6 The regiment _____ proudly along the high street.
7 Adam _____ over the low wall.
8 The snake _____ along the ground.
9 Paul _____ on the ice-covered path.

b Write the sentences, completing each with a word that means said. Use a different word each time.

1 'What time does the programme end?' she _____.
2 'Half past ten, madam,' the manager _____.
3 'We shall win this match easily,' the captain _____.
4 'You must let the cake cool before you put it in the tin,' she _____.
5 'It's my fault,' he _____. 'I accept full responsibility.'
6 'Get off!' the man _____ as the children climbed on to his gate.

c Write the sentences, replacing each underlined word with a stronger, more forceful word.

1 The car <u>bumped</u> into the tree.
2 I was <u>surprised</u> to find that the box was empty.
3 The children <u>smiled</u> at the antics of the clowns.
4 In his anger he <u>hit</u> a policeman.
5 The glass was <u>broken</u> into a thousand pieces.
6 The vandals <u>damaged</u> the building.

d Add a similar word to each of these groups.

1 weak fragile delicate infirm
2 roam ramble meander saunter
3 clasp hold grasp seize
4 funny comical amusing hilarious
5 tumult hubbub commotion turmoil
6 glistened sparkled shone glittered
7 hit bang knock beat
8 think meditate reflect ponder
9 fasten tie attach link
10 quick nimble agile energetic
11 drag pull tow heave
12 thieve swindle embezzle steal

e Make a list of words that seem to imitate or suggest the sounds associated with them – words such as crackle, bang, thud and plop.

Using words

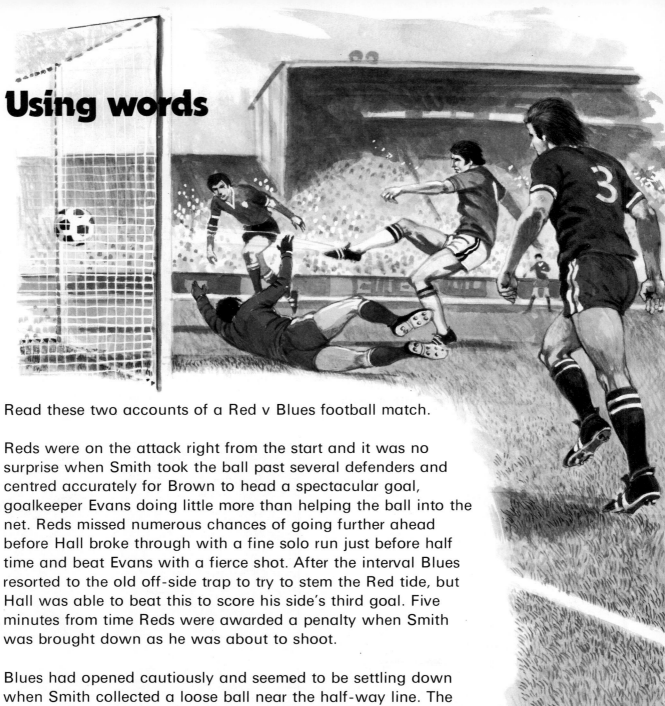

Read these two accounts of a Red v Blues football match.

Reds were on the attack right from the start and it was no surprise when Smith took the ball past several defenders and centred accurately for Brown to head a spectacular goal, goalkeeper Evans doing little more than helping the ball into the net. Reds missed numerous chances of going further ahead before Hall broke through with a fine solo run just before half time and beat Evans with a fierce shot. After the interval Blues resorted to the old off-side trap to try to stem the Red tide, but Hall was able to beat this to score his side's third goal. Five minutes from time Reds were awarded a penalty when Smith was brought down as he was about to shoot.

Blues had opened cautiously and seemed to be settling down when Smith collected a loose ball near the half-way line. The ball ran kindly for him and he was able to outpace several defenders who were clearly handicapped by the treacherous surface. From somewhere near the corner flag Smith lobbed the ball to Brown who opened the scoring despite the goalkeeper's valiant attempt to stop him. Blues steadied themselves and were unfortunate to fall further behind to an opportunist goal by Hall just before the interval. The second half saw Blues in determined mood, but their plans to get back into the game were thwarted when Hall was allowed to score again from what looked like an offside position. Further misfortune followed when Smith appeared to trip over a defender's outstretched leg and was awarded a penalty.

a Compare the two accounts and the way they use words. How are the two accounts alike? In what ways are they different? What do you think would be the loyalties of the people who wrote them and how has this influenced their view of the game? Which account do you think is more accurate?

b

1 Now write two contrasting accounts of what might happen at the end of a match, when some of the spectators move on to the pitch. In your first account show this as a good-natured and harmless display of enthusiasm and loyalty, with nobody getting hurt and the police moving in calmly only to make sure that the celebrations don't get out of hand.

In your second account of the same incident you must adopt a quite different viewpoint, showing the offending fans as a disorderly and drunken rabble who trespass on to the pitch in spite of all police efforts to stop them. Several scuffles follow.

2 Write two contrasting accounts of a fire at a block of flats. In the first, describe the rapid response of the fire brigade and the orderly way in which they set about their work, controlling the fire, evacuating the building and rescuing those who are trapped.

In your second account keep to the same broad outline, but make everything as dramatic and sensational as possible.

c

1 You have been away on a week's holiday when it rained steadily for the first four days. Then the sun came out. Write a cheerful account of the holiday, mentioning mostly the good points and the things you enjoyed.

Write a second account of the same holiday, chiefly complaining about the things that went wrong.

2 You are the manager of a company and you are presenting your annual report to the shareholders. The company has lost money, but you are optimistic about the future and look forward confidently to better times.

Then present a gloomy picture of the same situation, dwelling mostly on losses and misfortunes and giving little hope of early improvement.

d

1 Write two contrasting articles about fox-hunting – the first showing it as a skilled sport that gives pleasure to people, the second describing it as a cruel activity that ought to be banned.

2 Write two contrasting articles about the proposed extension of an airport near a town or city – one in favour listing all the benefits, the second opposing the plan, explaining the disadvantages that will follow.

e People sometimes say, 'It must be true; I saw it in print.' How true is this? How can we be sure about the truth of what we read? How far should a writer's point of view influence what he or she writes and how can we recognise this in what they have written?

Practice pages

a Alternative headings

Under what alternative headings could you look for information about these topics?

1	Mallard	9	Aqueduct
2	Barbados	10	Stonework
3	Hats	11	Runway
4	Plays	12	Guernsey
5	Pigs	13	Natterjack
6	Schooner	14	Air-conditioning
7	Wombat	15	Coyote
8	Oranges		

b *Oxford Junior Encyclopaedia* (see page 75)

In which volume would you look for these topics?

1	Money	7	Architecture
2	Sugar-beet	8	Tunnelling
3	Police	9	Reptiles
4	The Incas	10	Camping
5	Florence Nightingale	11	Newspapers
6	Nigeria	12	Nutrition

c *Children's Britannica* (see page 75)

In which volume would you look for the main entries about these topics?

1	Netball	7	Bees
2	Kangaroo	8	Bee-keeping
3	Uruguay	9	The Crusades
4	The Solar System	10	Roman roads
5	Housekeeping	11	Africa
6	Charles Darwin	12	Chess

d Write the sentences, completing each with a word that means said. Use a different word each time.

1 'Keep your voices low,' he _____. 'Somebody might hear us.'

2 'Here are the results of the competition,' she _____ .

3 'Oh please let me have it,' she _____ .

4 'Finally,' the producer _____, 'I would like to thank all those who have helped in any way.'

5 'Halt!' _____ the sentry. 'Identify yourself.'

e Write the sentences, replacing each underlined word with a stronger, more forceful word.

1 I was sure that I had the right answer.

2 The smuggled goods were taken by the police.

3 The soldiers were told to attack.

4 We were puzzled by the conjurer's tricks.

5 The cavalry raced towards the enemy guns.

f Write these headings in your note book or exercise book.

For younger readers   For older readers

Then write these titles (all fiction) under the correct heading.

The Stones of the Moon, The Clever Mouse, The Dream Dragon, Operation Midnight, Dolphin Island, The House that Sailed Away, The Fox Hole, The Good Tiger, Giant Kippernose and Other Stories, Sam Pig Goes to Market, Hounds of the King, A Kestrel for a Knave.

g Write these headings in your note book or exercise book:

Fiction　　Non-fiction

Then write these titles under the correct heading:

The Cuckoo Tree, The King of the Copper Mountain, Our World, The Dangerous Ones, A Family in Greece, The Vikings in Scotland, The First Men on the Moon, When the Wind Blows, Trouble on Sunday, Science and Crime Detection, Under the Sea, The Conjuror's Box.

h Combine these two accounts into one so as to cover the main points.

Saturn, the second largest planet in the solar system, is unique on account of the rings round it which, when seen through a telescope, make it one of the most beautiful objects in the sky. Because Saturn's axis is tilted we see the rings from different angles at different times. As well as the rings, Saturn has 10 moons, including Titan, the biggest satellite in the solar system. Saturn is such a long way from the sun that it takes $29\frac{1}{2}$ years to complete its orbit, as against one year for the earth.

Saturn is remarkable for the three flat rings that surround it at the level of its equator. These are composed of small particles of matter, and make the planet a spectacular sight. Saturn has 10 moons, the largest of which is the only satellite in the solar system with an atmosphere. Because of its great distance from the sun Saturn's year equals about $29\frac{1}{2}$ earth years, but a day on Saturn is only about $10\frac{1}{4}$ hours long because the planet spins on its axis more than twice as quickly as the earth does.

i How much can you remember?

Write a sentence for each answer.

1 What do we call a book or books containing information on many subjects?
2 What does the last volume of CHILDREN'S BRITANNICA consist of?
3 Which volume of OXFORD JUNIOR ENCYCLOPAEDIA deals with animals and plants?
4 Which volume of OXFORD JUNIOR ENCYCLOPAEDIA tells about the lives of some famous people?
5 Which of these items is arranged in alphabetical order: the Contents or the Index of a book?

j Add a similar word to each of these groups.

1 brilliant, shining, dazzling, gleaming
2 unhappy, mournful, downcast, sorrowful
3 impolite, rude, unmannerly, impudent
4 brave, courageous, fearless, valiant
5 angry, vexed, furious, irritated
6 constant, true, loyal, staunch
7 conquer, overcome, beat, vanquish
8 cry, yell, shriek, screech
9 impede, hinder, thwart, hamper
10 hurt, harm, wound, impair
11 spin, twirl, rotate, whirl
12 spring, leap, vault, bound

k Write the sentences, replacing each group of underlined words by one word.

1 The contents were set out at the front of the book.
2 The names in the index were arranged in alphabetical order.
3 The earth's path in space takes it round the sun once a year.
4 The stripes on a zebra seem to serve as protective coloration.
5 Some species of zebra are now no longer in existence.

Poetry

What is poetry? If you consult a dictionary it may tell you that poetry is the putting into words – especially in verse form – of our higher thoughts and feelings. Another definition is that poetry is language used in a special way so as to express our thoughts and communicate them to other people.

These special ways include the use of rhyme and metre and the choice and arrangements of words. Rhyme is the repetition of a sound, usually at the ends of lines but sometimes within lines. Metre means the rhythm of a poem and the way in which the beats or accents produce this. These features can be combined in various ways, but quite often a poem has no rhyme scheme and the metre may be irregular.

It is the choice and arrangement of words that especially distinguishes poetry from prose. It is here where the poet's imagination and feeling for words come into play. For example, a factual account of a pigeon would give the usual details of size, colour, flight, food and habits, but the poet sees these well-known birds as

Small blue busybodies
Strutting like fat gentlemen
With hands clasped
Under their swallowtail coats;
And, as they stump about,
Their heads like tiny hammers
Tap at imaginary nails
In non-existent walls.

a Write a sentence for each answer.

1 What are the special ways in which language is used in poetry?

2 What is rhyme?

3 What is metre?

4 What is it that especially distinguishes poetry from prose?

5 What would we expect to find in a factual account of a pigeon?

Write the words from the passage that mean the same as:

6 seek information from

7 tell or impart

8 joined together

9 pattern of rhymes (two words)

10 language that is not verse.

b Read the excerpt from *Pigeons* on page 86 and then answer the following questions.

1 How much information are we given about the size, colour, shape, posture and movement of pigeons?

2 Which words tell us that the birds move about in a rather stiff, pompous way?

3 Who have their hands clasped under their coats?

4 Why are the pigeons' heads compared to small hammers?

5 What imaginary items are mentioned in the poem?

c Here are some harder questions about the poem. This time the answers do not readily appear in the words of the poem, so you will have to work them out for yourself.

1 If the excerpt on page 86 had been written in a foreign language would you be able to tell that it was poetry and not prose? Give a reason for your answer.

2 What do you notice about the rhyme scheme or pattern of rhymes in the poem?

3 Which of these words could be used to describe the poem?
humorous, tragic, lively, fanciful, obscure, clear

4 Allowing for poetic imagination and expression would you say that the picture that the poem gives us is generally true or not true?

5 The poem is about birds, but which human attributes and characteristics are dealt with?

d Here are some excerpts from poems about other birds. Say what you think the bird is in each case.

1 It was the Rainbow gave thee birth,
And left thee all her lovely hues;

2 And, like a stroke of doom, drops down
and swoops across the empty hall,
and plucks a quick mouse off the stair . . .

3 The wrinkled sea beneath him crawls;
He watches from his mountain walls,
And like a thunderbolt he falls.

4 Higher still and higher
From the earth thou springest
Like a cloud of fire;
The blue deep thou wingest;
And singing still dost soar, and soaring ever singest.

e If you can get hold of it, read the complete poem *Pigeons* (it's by Richard Kell) and look for other images or word pictures about these birds.

Poetry

We have seen that the language of poetry is not so very different from any other except in the way it is used. Many of the poet's words will be those of everyday speech, although sometimes there will be need for words that have a deeper meaning. Other words are chosen for their sound as much as for their meaning. All play their part in helping the poet to create word pictures that both nourish and exercise the reader's imagination.

We all need this quality of imagination and we all use it to some extent. The poet uses it more than most of us and sets the results down in a form that we can all share. But the poem on its own is not enough. The reader must respond to bring the pictures to life. Thoughts and ideas put into a poem must take root and grow in the reader's mind. In this way we often find some extra quality in a poem each time we read it, while different readers may interpret the same poem differently.

Poems can offer us a wide variety of moods and themes. Sometimes they will merely amuse or comfort us, but often they will do much more than this. Poems can make us think deeply, so that instead of being an escape from the real world they are a way of seeing it more clearly and in a way made fresh by the poet's vision.

a   Write a sentence for each answer.

1   In what way is the language of poetry different from any other?
2   What else are words chosen for as well as for their meaning?
3   What do words help the poet to create?
4   Which quality does the poet use more than most of us?
5   A poem on its own is not enough. What else must happen?
6   What may happen each time we read a poem?
7   How may different readers react to the same poem?

Write the words from the passage that mean the same as:

8   act in return
9   explain the meaning of
10 ability to see things by imaginative thinking.

b   *The Sea*   by James Reeves

The sea is a hungry dog,
Giant and grey.
He rolls on the beach all day.
With his clashing teeth and shaggy jaws.
Hour upon hour he gnaws
The rumbling, tumbling stones,
And 'Bones, bones, bones, bones!'
The giant sea-dog moans,
Licking his greasy paws.

And when the night wind roars
And the moon rocks in the stormy cloud,
He bounds to his feet and snuffs and sniffs,
Shaking his wet sides over the cliffs,
And howls and hollos long and loud.

But on quiet days in May or June,
When even the grasses on the dune
Play no more their reedy tune,
With his head between his paws
He lies on the sandy shores,
So quiet, so quiet, he scarcely snores.

Read the poem several times and then write a plain language (prose) version, beginning something like this:

The sea is like a big, hungry dog that rolls about on the beach all day. . . .

Then compare the two versions. In what way are they alike? In what way are they different? Say which you think is more vivid and more effective, giving reasons for your decision.

c   Read the poem again and make lists of all the sounds and movements that are described or mentioned. Why do you think there are so many of them and how do they contribute to the over-all effect of the poem?

d   The sea, and things to do with the sea (such as ships, sailors, beaches, cliffs etc.) have always had a special fascination for poets. Write an essay suggesting why you think this is so.

e   Make a list of poems about the sea. Then choose one that particularly interests you and copy it (or part of it) in your note book or exercise book.

Poetry

The poet Coleridge once said that poetry was 'the best words in the best order'. This tells us a little about poetry, but not much. The best way of discovering the nature of poetry is to look at some examples and see how poets use words to describe things and convey the truth of what they see and feel.

Things in nature – such as birds, trees and flowers – and the passing of the seasons are often seen by poets with a new awareness and insight. Thus, in Autumn 'the rose tree's thread of scent draws thin', while in winter 'the wind gnaws with teeth of glass'. At night the stars 'freeze on the sky' while morning sees 'the first sharp splinters of dawn'. Holes in the roofs of deserted cottages are 'thatched with sunlight'; a beautiful Chinese girl has a face 'like yellow water', while a caterpillar 'tickles' a wall as it crawls along.

Many poems build up a picture by means of delicate touches and subtle effects, but others go for a bolder approach. The opening lines of *Daniel*, for example, make an immediate impact:

> Darius the Mede was a king and a wonder.
> His eye was proud, and his voice was thunder.
> He kept bad lions in a monstrous den.
> He fed up the lions on Christian men.

The poem sweeps into action at once and maintains its pace and vigour to the end.

a Write a sentence for each answer.

1 Who said that poetry was 'the best words in the best order'?
2 What is the best way of discovering the nature of poetry?
3 What sort of things are often seen by poets with a new awareness?
4 When does the rose tree's scent draw thin?
5 When does the wind blow 'with teeth of glass'?
6 Explain what is meant by 'the first sharp splinters of dawn'.
7 Explain how holes in a roof are 'thatched with sunlight'.
8 Explain how the caterpillar 'tickles' the wall.
9 How effective is the use of rhyme and rhythm in *Daniel*?
10 What picture of Darius do we get from the opening of *Daniel*?

b Write the words from the passage opposite that mean the same as

1 carry or impart
2 consciousness
3 deep understanding
4 abandoned
5 keeps up or upholds
6 strength, energy or power

c Here are a number of things that poets have written about together with the special words and phrases they have used to describe them. Write them out, re-arranging the right-hand column in the correct order.

1 a saucer of milk   like polished gold
2 a grey squirrel   like spun glass
3 snow   sudden fiery flowers
4 a thrush's eggs   a fish of the air
5 the moon   a creamy sea
6 inside a buttercup   four blue stones
7 fireworks   like swans asleep
8 a dragonfly's wings   a small grey coffee pot
9 old sailing ships   a child's balloon
10 a swallow   crystal manna

d Here are the opening lines of a poem called *The Highwayman*:

The wind was a torrent of darkness among the
    gusty trees.
The moon was a ghostly galleon tossed upon
    cloudy seas.
The road was a ribbon of moonlight over the
    purple moor.
And the highwayman came riding –
    Riding – riding –
The highwayman came riding, up to the
    old inn-door.

Compare this with *Daniel* on page 90. In what way are the two openings alike? In what ways are they different? How effective are they in setting the scene? Judging only by the titles and the opening lines what kind of action and events would you expect to follow?

e Make a list of things in nature, such as those mentioned on page 90, that poets have written about. Then choose one nature poem that particularly interests you and copy it (or part of it) in your note book or exercise book.

Books for young readers

Every year thousands of new children's books are published. They are written specially to inform and entertain young readers, taking account of their needs and interests.

If we go back about two hundred years, however, we find a very different picture. Then, there were not many books of any sort available, so it is not surprising that few of them were made specially for the young. Books available to children might include the Bible, stories of saints and martyrs, Aesop's fables and perhaps a few tales about King Arthur, Robin Hood and the Trojan War. Books such as *Pilgrim's Progress* and *Robinson Crusoe* were read by children, although they had not been specially written for them.

When people began to write for children they thought mostly of giving instructions about manners and behaviour and it was not until 1744 that anyone produced a book that was intended to entertain as well. In that year John Newbery published *A Little Pretty Pocket-Book*, a little book containing fables in verse, descriptions of games and a rhyming alphabet.

During Queen Victoria's reign children's books began to look more like those of to-day, and some of the outstanding works of the time, such as *Alice's Adventures in Wonderland, Black Beauty, Treasure Island* and *The Jungle Books* are still enjoyed to-day.

a Write a sentence for each answer.

1 How many new children's books are published each year?

2 What sort of things do books for children take account of?

3 What books might be available to children about 200 years ago?

4 Name two books that were read by children although not specially written for them.

5 What sort of things did the first children's books include?

6 What was different about *A Little Pretty Pocket-Book*?

7 When and by whom was *A Little Pretty Pocket-Book* published?

8 Mention some of the contents of *A Little Pretty Pocket-Book*.

9 When did children's books begin to look more like those of to-day?

10 Mention some outstanding books of the Victorian age that are still read to-day.

b Here are a number of categories of books and a specimen title belonging to each. Write them out, re-arranging the right-hand column in the correct order.

1 Myths and legends — The Phoenix and the Carpet

2 Historical novel — Supernatural Tales of Terror and Suspense

3 Animal story — Jennings and Darbishire

4 Fantasy and magic — Irish Sagas and Folk-Tales

5 Detective story — Gulliver's Travels

6 Humour — Tarka the Otter

7 School story — A Hundred Million Francs

8 Space adventure — Bowman of Crécy

9 Ghost stories — Threshold of the Stars

10 Adult story, adapted — Professor Branestawm up the Pole

c Here are brief descriptions of some well-known books. Write their titles.

1 The story of Tom, a little chimney sweep who was badly treated. After falling in a river he lives in the sea, becoming a kind of miniature merman. The story is thus partly realistic and partly fantastic.

2 A story of four sisters – Meg, Jo, Beth and Amy March – growing up in New England at the time of the American Civil War.

3 The autobiography of a horse, the story tells of the cruel treatment that the animal receives from a succession of owners. The book was written partly as a plea for the humane treatment of animals

4 Several stories about the adventures of a human baby who is adopted by Mother Wolf and brought up in the ways of the jungle.

5 The adventures of Mole, Water Rat, Badger and Mr Toad. They speak and often behave as humans do, but they keep some animal characteristics as well. Many of the incidents centre round the wayward Mr Toad and the attempts of his friends to keep him out of trouble.

d Choose one or two books that you have read and write brief summaries of them, as above.

e Write the names of any books written by these authors:

Joan Aiken
René Guillot
C. S. Lewis
Hugh Lofting
William Mayne
E. Nesbit
Mary Norton
Willard Price

Arthur Ransome
Noel Streatfield
Rosemary Sutcliffe
Geoffrey Trease
Henry Treece
Alison Uttley
Ronald Welch
Ian Serraillier.

Myths

The word myth comes from the Greek word 'mythos' meaning speech or talk, which reminds us that these ancient traditional tales of gods and heroes came about through the spoken word long before they were written down.

Nowadays we probably look upon myths merely as stories, and it is true that they are well worth reading from that point of view alone. But the beginnings of myths may have been rooted in old religious or magical rites. Perhaps people believed that by 'acting-out' or performing certain rituals they could make happen the things they wanted to happen. At this stage there would be no intention of making up stories or poems to entertain people.

Another explanation of the origins of myths is that they were an attempt to explain things that people could not understand. We know that there are no such things as monsters or other supernatural beings, but such things may have helped primitive peoples to communicate their feelings about the mystery of life and why we are here.

In time some of the early beliefs and practices became embodied in various tales and poems, and eventually someone decided to write them down. The writers may have changed some of the detail and we know that some parts have been lost. But enough remains to provide us with a rich and varied literary heritage.

a Write a sentence for each answer.

1 What is the origin and meaning of the word myth?

2 Did myths begin with the spoken or the written word?

3 Suggest a reason why people carried out certain rituals.

4 What other explanation is there of the origins of myths?

5 What purpose may have been served by stories about monsters or other supernatural beings?

6 What may have happened to the old stories when they came to be written down?

Write the words from the passage that mean the same as:

7 handed down from generation to generation

8 firmly established

9 solemn ceremonies or observances

10 included or incorporated.

b Here is a story from Norse mythology. It tells of the theft of Thor's hammer, one of the most important of all the treasures of the gods. Write it out as five sentences, putting in all necessary capital letters and punctuation.

the gods and the giants were often quarrelling and fighting with each other one day the giant thrym stole thors hammer demanding the goddess freya as the price of its return freya refused to marry thrym and so an alternative way of recovering the hammer had to be found at last someone suggested that thor dressed up as freya should go to giantland as if prepared to marry thrym thor reluctantly agreed and thrym laid out a great feast for his expected bride but as soon as thor got his hands on his hammer he revealed himself and killed all the giants who were there that day

c Write this story from Greek mythology, choosing the correct word from each pair in brackets.

According to Greek mythology Pandora was the first (man, woman) on earth. She had been given a box which the gods warned her not to open. In time, however, she was (overcome, surrounded) by (laziness, curiosity) and (regularly, finally) (lifted, lowered) the lid. All the troubles and (problems, advantages) that now (benefit, afflict) mankind flew out. As (quickly, slowly) as she could Pandora (opened, shut) the lid, just in time to (prevent, allow) the escape of Hope.

d To which countries or people do these mythical characters belong?

| Apollo | Jupiter | Siegfried |
| Finn | Vishnu | Osiris |

e Write two or three sentences about each of these mythical monsters:

1 Argus
2 Cerberus
3 Chimera
4 Cyclops
5 Fenrir (or Fenris-wolf)
6 Harpies
7 Hydra
8 Jormungard
9 Medusa
10 Minotaur.

Practice page

a Poetry or prose?

Say which of these items would be more suitable subjects for poetry and which you think would be better expressed in prose.

1 A recipe for steak and kidney pudding.

2 A description of a walk along a deserted beach.

3 A message for the milkman, ordering an extra bottle.

4 A note to your teacher explaining your absence from school.

5 An impression of the pictures and patterns that the clouds sometimes seem to make.

6 A road test of a motor vehicle.

7 A description of the rain beating against the windows of a house.

8 Some ideas of what a dog may think about as it lies in front of the fire.

9 The thoughts of an old sailor as he sits on the quayside, watching the boats come and go.

10 An official report of a collision between two oil tankers off the south coast.

b Here are the titles of some books written for young people. Suggest what you think each story is about.

1 A Midsummer Night's Death
2 Captain Cobweb's Cowboys
3 The Children's Crusade
4 Steam on the Line
5 The Edge of the Cloud
6 Run for Your Life
7 Goals in the Air
8 Boy Astronaut
9 The Foundling
10 The Borribles

c Here are brief descriptions of some more well-known books. Write their titles.

1 The story of a boy who refuses to grow up. He and the Darling children visit Never-Never Land where they have adventures with Captain Hook (a pirate), a crocodile and an Indian princess.

2 The story of a ship's surgeon who is the only survivor of a shipwreck. He swims ashore and finds himself in a strange land where the people are only 15 cm high. In later voyages he encounters a race of giants, a flying island and some talking horses.

3 The story of a man who was shipwrecked on an uninhabited island where he lived alone for many years. At length he meets another human being – a young native whom he rescues from cannibals.